Domestic Workers Talk

LANGUAGE AT WORK

Series Editors: **Jo Angouri**, *University of Warwick, UK* and **Rebecca Piekkari**, *Aalto University Business School, Finland*

Language at Work is a new series designed to bring together scholars interested in workplace research. The modern workplace has changed significantly in recent years. The international nature of business activities and the increasing rate of mobility around the world create a new challenging environment for individuals and organisations alike. The advancements in technology have reshaped the ways employees collaborate at the interface of linguistic, national and professional borders. The complex linguistic landscape also results in new challenges for health care systems and legal settings. This and other phenomena around the world of work have attracted significant interest; it is still common however for relevant research to remain within clear disciplinary and methodological boundaries.

The series aims to create space for exchange of ideas and dialogue and seeks to explore issues related to power, leadership, politics, teamwork, culture, ideology, identity, decision making and motivation across a diverse range of contexts, including corporate, health care and institutional settings. *Language at Work* welcomes mixed methods research and it will be of interest to researchers in linguistics, international management, organisation studies, sociology, medical sociology and decision sciences.

All books in this series are externally peer-reviewed.

Full details of all the books in this series and of all our other publications can be found on http://www.multilingual-matters.com, or by writing to Multilingual Matters, St Nicholas House, 31-34 High Street, Bristol, BS1 2AW, UK.

LANGUAGE AT WORK: 9

Domestic Workers Talk

Language Use and Social Practices in a Multilingual Workplace

Kellie Gonçalves and Anne Ambler Schluter

MULTILINGUAL MATTERS
Bristol • Jackson

DOI https://doi.org/10.21832/GONCAL6758
Library of Congress Cataloging in Publication Data
A catalog record for this book is available from the Library of Congress.
Names: Gonçalves, Kellie, author. | Schluter, Anne Ambler, author.
Title: Domestic Workers Talk: Language Use and Social Practices in a
    Multilingual Workplace/Kellie Gonçalves and Anne Ambler Schluter.
Description: Bristol; Jackson: Multilingual Matters, [2024] | Series:
    Language at Work: 9 | Includes bibliographical references and index. |
    Summary: "Set in a multilingual cleaning company that serves Anglophone
    customers in the upper-(middle) class suburbs of New York City, this
    book presents an ethnographic study into power, language policy and
    communication from the perspectives of the Brazilian-American employer
    as well as the company's Hispanophone and Lusophone employees"--
    Provided by publisher.
Identifiers: LCCN 2023029152 (print) | LCCN 2023029153 (ebook) | ISBN
    9781800416741 (paperback) | ISBN 9781800416758 (hardback) | ISBN
    9781800416772 (epub) | ISBN 9781800416765 (pdf)
Subjects: LCSH: Household employees--Social conditions. |
    Multilingualism--Economic aspects.
Classification: LCC HD6072 .G65 2024 (print) | LCC HD6072 (ebook) | DDC
    331.4/12791--dc23/eng/20230919
LC record available at https://lccn.loc.gov/2023029152
LC ebook record available at https://lccn.loc.gov/2023029153

British Library Cataloguing in Publication Data
A catalogue entry for this book is available from the British Library.

ISBN-13: 978-1-80041-675-8 (hbk)
ISBN-13: 978-1-80041-674-1 (pbk)

Multilingual Matters
UK: St Nicholas House, 31-34 High Street, Bristol, BS1 2AW, UK.
USA: Ingram, Jackson, TN, USA.

Website: https://www.multilingual-matters.com
Twitter: Multi_Ling_Mat
Facebook: https://www.facebook.com/multilingualmatters
Blog: https://www.channelviewpublications.wordpress.com

Copyright © 2024 Kellie Gonçalves and Anne Ambler Schluter.

All rights reserved. No part of this work may be reproduced in any form or by any means without permission in writing from the publisher.

The policy of Multilingual Matters/Channel View Publications is to use papers that are natural, renewable and recyclable products, made from wood grown in sustainable forests. In the manufacturing process of our books, and to further support our policy, preference is given to printers that have FSC and PEFC Chain of Custody certification. The FSC and/or PEFC logos will appear on those books where full certification has been granted to the printer concerned.

Typeset by Deanta Global Publishing Services, Chennai, India.

To Magda and all of Shine's employees.

And to Janet Holmes, whose work on language, gender and the workplace sparked our curiosity and inspired our research on Shine.

Contents

	Figures and Tables	xi
	Acknowledgments	xiii
1	Introduction	1
	1.1 Introduction	1
	1.2 Domestic Labor and the Global 'Female' Care Chain	5
	1.3 Domestic Labor in the US	10
	1.4 Newark, Elizabeth and Westwood: Setting the Scene	11
	1.5 Multilingual Communities, a Multilingual Company and Power	19
	1.6 Overview of Chapters	20
2	Advancing Methodology: Using a Mixed Methodological Approach within a Multilingual Cleaning Company	24
	2.1 Introduction	24
	2.2 A Vignette by Kellie: My Memory of Magda as a Teenager	25
	2.3 Research Design: Exploratory and Systematic Phases of Our Study	27
	2.4 Data: Data Collection and Data Triangulation	31
	2.5 Poststructuralist Perspectives and Epistemological Shifts within Sociolinguistics: Employing Mobile, Critical and Post-Critical Ethnography	32
	2.6 Mobile Ethnography: A Case of Co-Present Immersion and Sustained Engagement with Participants	34
	2.7 Critical and Post-Critical Ethnography: Interpretive Stances, Reflexivity and Positionality	36
	2.8 Temporality within Ethnography: The Longitudinal Aspects of Our Study	37
	2.9 Chapter Summary	38

3   Magda: The Personal and Professional Trajectory of Shine's
    Owner   40
    3.1   Introduction   40
    3.2   Tracing Magda's History: From Childhood up to Her
          Formative Years   41
    3.3   Life-Changing Experiences and Young Adulthood: Family
          Tragedy, A Scholarship and Moving to the City   43
    3.4   Transnational Migration and Private Language Planning:
          Magda's Own Domestic Worker Experience in the US   44
    3.5   From Nanny to Entrepreneur: The Hegemonic
          Discourse of Learning English: The Key to Magda's
          Upward Social Mobility and Professional Identities   45
    3.6   Leadership, Empathy and Emotional Intelligence:
          'The Softer Side' of Magda   50
    3.7   Emotional Intelligence: A Model to Understand Magda's
          Leadership Style at Shine   52
    3.8   Mediation: The Case of Magda's Multilingual and
          Intercultural Competence   63
    3.9   Company-External Communication: A Language Policy
          for Customers   71
    3.10 Chapter Summary   76

4   The Interplay between Identity, Ideology and Capital that
    Strengthens Cultural Attachments: The Pull of Portuguese
    and the Portuguese-Centric Ironbound Community for Shine's
    Hispanophone Employees   79
    4.1   Introduction   79
    4.2   The Shifting Dynamics of Capital and Migration:
          The Conditions for Emergent Cultural-Linguistic
          Orientations toward Non-Dominant Groups   81
    4.3   An Introduction to this Chapter's Primary Participants   83
    4.4   Some Linguistic Context: A Brief Comparison of
          Portuguese vs. Spanish Phonology   84
    4.5   Setting the Scene: Capital, Neoliberalism and
          the Extended Ironbound Community   85
    4.6   The Mechanics of Fitting in Linguistically:
          Dual-Linguality or Accommodation to Shine's
          Portuguese-Centric Orientation?   87
    4.7   Analyzing Orientations to Portuguese-Centricity
          Beyond the Shine Community of Practice: A Focus on
          Ideology and Identity   94
    4.8   Putting It All Together: Capital, Identity, Ideology,
          Agency and Diasporic Belonging   97
    4.9   Chapter Summary   98

5   Multicompetence as Essential and English-Language
    Proficiency as Secondary: Examining the Shape of Customer–
    Employee Interactions between Speakers who do not Share
    a Common Language   100
    5.1 Introduction   100
    5.2 Linguistic and Extra-Linguistic Resources within the
         Multilingual Workplace   103
    5.3 Lusophone Perspectives for Analysis: The Cases of
         Marcela, Maria Clara and Adriana   103
    5.4 The Use of Artifacts, Gestures and Language to Convey
         Meaning   105
    5.5 Multicompetence, Digital Technologies and Diminished
         Investment   109
    5.6 Reflections on Multimodality with Respect to
         the Preceding Analyses   111
    5.7 Chapter Summary   113

6   Conclusion   114
    6.1 Communication Practices at a Migrant-Run,
         Multilingual Blue-Collar Workplace: Reflections
         on Emergent Themes and their Contributions to
         the Literature   114
    6.2 English, Intercultural Competence, Language Policy,
         Power, Diasporic Belonging, Migrant Entrepreneurship
         and the Decentering of Language   116
    6.3 Magda: A Complex Portrait of a Powerful, Emotionally
         Intelligent Migrant Entrepreneur   118
    6.4 Hispanophone Employees' Fit within Shine and
         the Larger Portuguese-Centric Ironbound Community:
         Observations about Investment and Implications for
         Language and Diaspora Research   120
    6.5 Insights into the Importance of English Based
         on Findings from the Shine Context   123
    6.6 The Status of Shine Today   125
    6.7 Learning from Shine: Implications for Future Studies   127

    References   129
    Index   143

Figures and Tables

Figures

Figure 1.1	Shine's company hierarchy with Magda located at the top	2
Figure 1.2	Global care work and organizational divisions (adapted from Gonçalves & Schluter, 2020)	6
Figure 1.3	Key factors considered when working with Shine's migrant female domestic workers	9
Figure 1.4	Portuguese flags decorating shops on Ferry Street	12
Figure 1.5	Ferry Street also known as Portugal Avenue	13
Figure 1.6	Written varieties of Portuguese and Spanish on a shop window in the Ironbound	14
Figure 1.7–1.8	Pictures of homes in the Ironbound neighborhood	16
Figure 1.9–1.10	Pictures of homes in Westwood	17
Figure 1.11	Gap Kids in downtown Westwood	18
Figure 1.12	Williams-Sonoma in downtown Westwood	18
Figure 3.1	The cleaning company hierarchy: Magda is at the top of the hierarchy, where company values and job instructions trickle down to her employees. Of the four Spanish-speaking employees, three are from Ecuador and one is from Honduras	64

Tables

Table 2.1	Methodological advantages and challenges of embarking on this kind of study	30
Table 2.2	Mixed methods and data sets used in this study	34
Table 3.1	Emotional Intelligence according to Goleman's (1998, 2000, 2015) five features	53
Table 4.1	Descriptive data about the four Shine employees whose interview data inform this chapter	83

Acknowledgments

This book has taken us longer to write than we had originally envisioned. One of the reasons has to do with the fact that our research on Shine had always been a small side project for both of us. It all started in 2010 when Kellie read a passage by Janet Holmes about the methodological challenges of accessing blue-collar workplaces, which she found intriguing yet problematic. Within months, we met each other at an international conference in Switzerland and, before long, we learned that in addition to our penchant for running, yoga and *pão de queijo*, we were both from New Jersey, US, and speakers of English, Portuguese and Spanish: it seemed like the perfect match to carry out a larger research project on Shine, which Kellie had access to and so our collaborative journey began in late 2010.

In 2015, we presented a part of this work at the International Symposium on Bilingualism (ISB) at Rutgers University in New Jersey, which is located not too far from the research site. This meant that we could bring some locally based research to this international conference. Although the audience was sparse, Helen Kelly-Holmes, who at the time, was also co-editor of the journal *Language Policy* (together with Ofelia García) approached us after our presentation and suggested we write an article for the journal on Magda, Shine's owner and main language broker. Not long afterward we were contacted by Jo Angouri, who inquired if we'd be interested in writing up a book about Shine for her then-new series titled *Language at Work* for Multilingual Matters. Needless to say, we were both flattered and excited by these opportunities to share our work with fellow researchers, peers and students.

Over the years we have given several presentations at international conferences and invited workshops about the multilingual practices at Shine from different perspectives, and we are extremely grateful for the constructive feedback we have received from critical audience members, colleagues, friends and students along the way. Our (2017) work on Magda as the primary language broker was key to this project and we have been pleasantly surprised by individual reactions to Magda, especially from students. We have received emails from instructors and students from different parts of the world inquiring about Magda and Shine. This response was at once astonishing but also welcome. We realized that what we had found at Shine in terms of language practices was not only worth reporting on and expanding, but, it also seemed like somewhat of an anomaly within the field of sociolinguistics and multilingual studies at the time. Finally, after several years of working on this project together, we are pleased that it is now in its published format. We hope that the book's content will continue to intrigue colleagues and students alike who are concerned with multilingual matters, language and workplace studies, transnational migration, ethnic economies and the female-gendered nature of domestic labor in particular.

Co-writing a book requires time, patience, countless discussions about what to include and exclude as well as an outstanding support network both professionally and personally. Indeed, we would like to thank Magda, her employees and several customers of Shine, all of whom allowed us to talk to them and observe them for hours, days and at times, even months over several consecutive years. Without their participation and goodwill, this book would not have been possible. *Muito obrigada!*

Over the years, we have received so much support in a myriad of ways at different times during this project from wonderful and critical colleagues, who we would like to thank. In no particular order, thank you to Janet Holmes, Jo Angouri, Helen Kelly-Holmes, Ofelia García, Barbara Johnstone, David Britain, Crispin Thurlow, Robert Blackwood, Elana Shohamy, Lourdes Ortega, Annick De Houwer, Unn Røyneland, Elizabeth Lanza, Pia Lane, Rafael Lomeu Gomes, Haley De Korne, Olga Solovova, Alastair Pennycook, Kristin Vold Lexander, Marilyn Martin-Jones, David Divita, Tamah Sherman, Sari Pietikäinen, Maiju Strömmer, Beatriz P. Lorente, Anna Kaiper-Marquez, Sinfree Makoni, Daniel Schreier, Christiane Meierkord, Edgar W. Schneider, Beatrix Busse, Monika Dannerer, Aneta Pavlenko, Monica Heller, Bonnie McElhinney, Adam Jaworski, Nic Guinto, Tommaso M. Milani, Carmen Rosa Caldas-Coulthard, Hugo Bowles, Alessia Cogo and Hans J. Ladegaard. We would also like to thank Livia Ganzella for her time, energy and assistance with the Portuguese transcriptions. Kellie would also like to thank Federico Erba for his assistance with the final stages of manuscript preparation. Kellie and Anne would both like to thank Zhou Yuan, Zoe, Federico Erba and Forugh Esmaeili for their work and assistance with the index. Kellie would also like to thank Núbia for helping with the final index.

At Multilingual Matters, we would like to thank Jo Angouri, the series editor, for giving us the opportunity to write up this book. Thank you, Jo, for your patience and expertise. Thank you, too, for giving us the time necessary to complete this manuscript. We would also like to extend a big thanks to Anna Roderick, whose professionalism and tremendous patience have been remarkable while guiding us throughout this book's project. Thank you very much for not giving up on us! We would also like to thank Flo McClelland, who greatly assisted us with the final stages of the production process.

We would also like to thank Springer, Mouton de Gruyter and Elsevier for permission to reprint material included in our book.

Longitudinal research projects are also only possible due to generous funding. Kellie is greatly indebted to the Bern University Research Foundation (17/2012), who generously funded all costs for an international conference, where parts of this project were presented.

On a more personal note, Kellie would like to thank her family, mom, dad, Ananias, Magda, Jen, Alois and Núbia for their tremendous support, patience and keeping me grounded with their good humor and fun family gatherings. Kellie is especially grateful to Alois and Núbia during the book's final stages when her 'alone time' was crucial and unquestioningly granted. Anne would like to thank Sasha, who unwittingly ended up spending a few vacations with Shine's employees through Anne's writing. She would also like to thank Eric Wolman for his continued insights into the customer side of the relationship between Brazilian domestic workers and the Anglophone homeowners they serve. Anne would also like to express her sincere gratitude to Magda for hosting her during data collection trips. Her extremely high level of generosity has yet to be matched by any other host.

1 Introduction

1.1 Introduction

This book presents an ethnographic study about a multilingual cleaning company, which we call 'Shine'. Shine is run by an American-Brazilian woman, Magda, who employs solely Portuguese- and Spanish-speaking migrant women to carry out domestic services for an elite and primarily Anglophone customer base located in Westwood, New Jersey, a very affluent suburb of New York City, US. Our aim with this book is to gain insights about society, language values, language policies, multilingual and multimodal embodied practices within a domestic labor context contributing diverse insights about real-world language use and embodied practices, social relations, power asymmetries and feminine-gendered workplace hierarchies. Because language practices within the context of domestic labor is a relatively under-researched area of language contact within the fields of applied linguistics, sociolinguistics and multilingual studies (Gonçalves & Schluter, 2020; Kaiper-Marquez & Makoni, 2022; Lorente, 2017), we hope our book sheds light on the complex and multilayered processes located at the intersection of communication and domestic labor. We have written this book for scholars in the fields of applied linguistics, sociolinguistics and multilingual studies; however, we also hope that this book will appeal to a different readership, including migrant business managers and entrepreneurs and policymakers. The major themes addressed in this book will be relevant to scholars, managers and practitioners since they include an investigation of:

(1) asymmetrical power dynamics and social class relations between employers and employees (depicted in Figure 1.1);
(2) language ideologies and the symbolic value of languages within certain language regimes;
(3) the multimodal and embodied ways in which communication is achieved between individuals who do not always share a common 'language';
(4) skillful deployment of resources and post-humanist applied linguistics;
(5) language policy and management within an all-female migrant workplace;

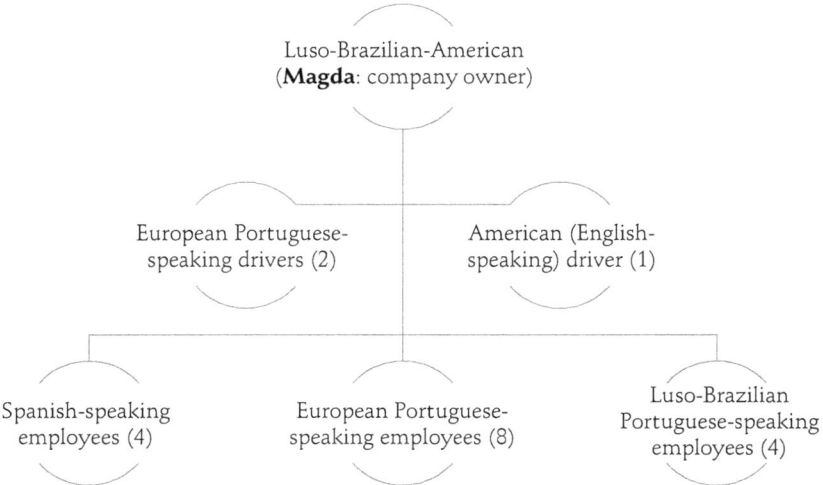

Figure 1.1 Shine's company hierarchy with Magda located at the top

(6) an under-researched and vulnerable group of women, namely, transnational domestic workers;
(7) the multifaceted identities of a migrant female business owner and successful entrepreneur;
(8) emotional intelligence and leadership style;
(9) the methodological approaches taken to understand and justify our representation and interpretation of how Shine is managed and functions from a sociolinguistic and political-economic perspective.

This book is highly influenced by poststructuralist perspectives and a broader epistemological shift that accounts for critical and ethnographic approaches within the field of sociolinguistics. In line with 'critical-constructivist sociolinguistics', we understand language as a 'social practice with speakers drawing on all kinds of linguistic resources for their own purposes' (Bell, 2014: 9), which include specific communicative practices, repertoires, 'bits of language' (Blommaert, 2010) as well as – and often in conjunction with – other semiotic means and artifacts (Gonçalves, 2020a; Kusters, 2021; Kusters *et al.*, 2017; Otsuji & Pennycook, 2015; Schluter, 2021; Schneider & Theyd, forthcoming; Theodoropoulou, 2020) resonating with post-humanist linguistics. In these ways, our work aligns with the recent paradigm shift in sociolinguistics, where the deployment of semiotic resources, of which one is language, allows for a richer, more complex understanding of communicative practices within a multilingual setting.

For reasons of clarity and entry into some of these academic debates, we provide a glimpse into a few of these salient themes via specific data extracts. We do this first and foremost to provide readers with the necessary contextual background about Magda, Shine's company hierarchy, its employees and its customers and the ways in which communication is managed and achieved between these diverse groups of people. We begin with Figure 1.1 and Shine's company hierarchy and organizational structure.

Figure 1.1 depicts Shine's workplace hierarchy with Magda, Shine's owner located at the top. From this figure we also see that the majority of Shine's workers are European Portuguese-speaking migrant women while the minority are Luso-Brazilian and Spanish speakers. In our study Magda openly states her preference for European Portuguese-speaking domestic workers due to their subordinate position and apparent ability to comply with Magda's orders and requests, which is highlighted in Extract (1):

Extract (1)

1. Magda: I mean, I'm very demanding and erm I think working with the Portuguese erm, I
2. actually, I like to work with the Portuguese better than erm with the Brazilians erm you know,
3. whatever I tell them to do, they are, you know, more accept, they accept it better

(Magda, Shine's owner)

As a result of Magda's preferences, Shine is comprised of a majority of European Portuguese-speaking staff, where European Portuguese becomes *the* language used for company-internal purposes between Magda and her employees and among employees for inter-employee communication. As such, European Portuguese also carries the highest symbolic value that is imbued with cultural capital within Shine on both a local and regional level despite its minority status within a US context. It may come as no surprise, therefore, that Shine's European Portuguese speakers are also in a privileged position in both their local communities (where European Portuguese prevails) and workplace in that they do not necessarily have to accommodate to their Spanish-speaking co-workers. We see this in Extract (2) by Dona Aura, a European Portuguese-speaking employee who admits to 'always' speaking Portuguese:

Extract (2)

1. Kellie: *Você usa mais o espanhol ou cê sempre fala o português [com as meninas?]* (do you use more Spanish or do you always speak in *Portuguese* [with the girls?])
2. Dona Aura: *Não, eu sempre falo o português* (No, I always speak *Portuguese*)
(Dona Aura, employee who has worked for Shine for 13 years)

While Shine's employees do not always share a common language among one another, we found that Spanish speakers and also the minority speakers of Shine usually accommodate to European Portuguese speakers for communication to be achieved. This is not the case, however, among Shine's employees and Shine's customer base, who are primarily Anglophones and thus English speakers. Despite not having a lingua franca to communicate in, we found that individuals either communicated via Magda as the main 'language broker' (Gonçalves & Schluter, 2017) or through multimodal and embodied practice as we see in Extract (3) with Mrs Malloy, a longtime customer of Shine:

Extract (3)

1. Mrs Malloy: This week we're not going to clean the windows and I'll point to the window and I'll
2. say, 'I:::'ve h:::ad them a::ll clea:::ned they're fi:::ne, you:: don't nee::d to touch them, so they're
3. a:::ll fi:::ne' like (laughter) and we do hand signals so and I say, 'do you under- ok?' and she's like
4. 'ok' and I don't know if that means 'yes, I understand you' or 'ok, you've said something' you
5. know? I, that, there is no like, there is no real verbal communication back

(Mrs Malloy, long-standing customer of Shine of 12 years)

Extract (3) is a prime example of how we cannot ignore embodied practice and the multimodal constitution of language in use. It also represents a common-sense view of language and society, what counts as 'real' language and who counts as a 'legitimate speaker' (Bourdieu, 1991). For Mrs Malloy and other customers, but also for some of Shine's own employees, *real* language is considered linguistic and verbal. Individuals' emic perspectives of being able to *really speak* a language is often correlated to complete mastery that is usually measured by a standard yardstick and marked by a particular accent rather than a combination of linguistic and non-linguistic or even semiotic repertoires (Gonçalves, 2020a; Gumperz, 1982; Kusters *et al.*, 2017, 2021; Otsuji & Pennycook, 2015; Rymes, 2014). How linguistic, communicative and semiotic repertoires are drawn on and used also raises relevant issues of how social meaning is co-constructed and negotiated in interaction.

On the basis of these extracts, which highlight several themes addressed throughout this book, we hope to have provided readers with a preview of what is to come throughout the remaining chapters that follow. In the next section, we focus on the topic of domestic labor globally and then within the US in order to situate our discussion within a national context. Afterwards, we describe the sites of Newark, Elizabeth and

Westwood in terms of their socioeconomic, ethnic, racial and linguistic makeup. These towns are where Shine's domestic workers reside, where customers and Magda live and also where Shine's headquarters is located.

1.2 Domestic Labor and the Global 'Female' Care Chain

In this section, we discuss domestic labor and the global 'female' chain before narrowing down our focus to domestic labor within an American context, where this study has been carried out. The reasons for this are threefold. First, we want to familiarize readers with the care work industry and more specifically, the domain of domestic work, which is often confined to the informal economy. Second, it is important to inform readers that domestic work is largely done by women and more specifically, transnational migrant women and/or women of color. Third, we want to highlight that domestic workers as a vulnerable group of women are under-represented within the new division of labor (Romero *et al.*, 2014) and therefore, also an under-represented context within academia, including the field of sociolinguistics (cf. Kaiper-Marquez & Makoni, 2022).

Domestic work is largely considered 'women's work' and thus highly feminine-gendered. To date the transfer of female labor within the *global care chain* (Hochschild, 2000) has grown to comprise 'the largest labor market worldwide' (Lutz, 2011: 15). Currently, women constitute approximately half of the world's migrant population; moreover, migrant women involved in the Global Care Chain account for the single largest female occupational group migrating globally (Gonçalves & Schluter, 2020; ILO, 2013, 2017; Kaiper-Marquez & Makoni, 2022; Lorente, 2017; Romero *et al.*, 2014).

For the purposes of this study, we are concerned with cleaning services and cleaning personnel in private home settings, referred to as domestic labor as seen in Figure 1.2, which outlines the organizational divisions within care work on a global scale. According to the International Labor Organization (ILO; 2020), 'domestic workers comprise a significant part of the global workforce in informal employment and are among the most vulnerable groups of workers'. Worldwide, there are approximately 67 million domestic workers (and over 100 million including undocumented workers), 80% of whom are women, resulting in a highly feminized sector. Despite the high numbers of domestic workers internationally, they are an underrepresented group within the new global division of labor (Romero *et al.*, 2014).

In an attempt to account for the underrepresentation of domestic workers, we also need to bear in mind that domestic work (and workers) are closely and complexly connected to (1) informal labor markets that result from the larger sociopolitical and economic development of the global care chain, (2) methodological challenges, i.e. accessing

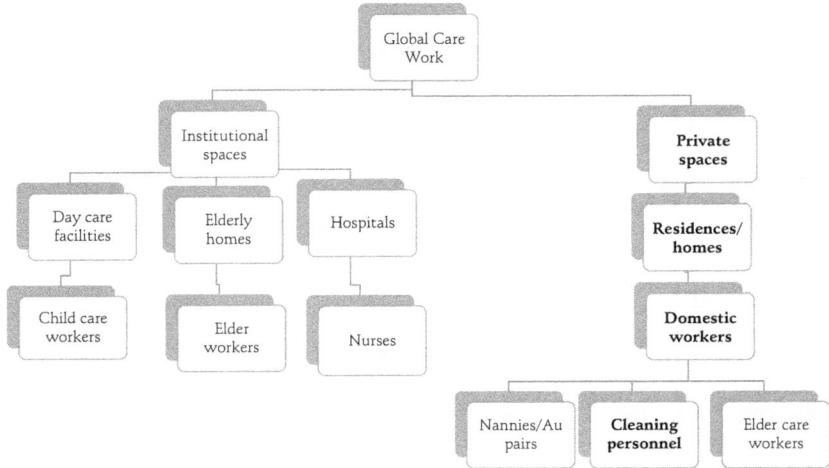

Figure 1.2 Global care work and organizational divisions (adapted from Gonçalves & Schluter, 2020)

(vulnerable) participants, many of whom are transnational migrant women, who may lack legal citizenship and/or the ability to communicate in the language of the host society and (3) domestic workers' physical workplaces, which simultaneously serve as private homes and are beyond the purview of state-regulation and public scrutiny. Next, we discuss each of these points in turn.

1.2.1 Transnational labor migration within domestic labor contexts

As previously stated, the transfer of female labor within the *global care chain* (Hochschild, 2000) has grown to comprise 'the largest labor market worldwide' (Lutz, 2011: 15). This is quite remarkable within the context of an already globalized world. Currently, we are experiencing a so-called 'crisis' society (Campos *et al.*, 2021) where instability prevails, and questions of citizenship and socioeconomic status help to determine individuals' movement across different borders. While Covid-19 caused an elongated period of immobility for many people worldwide, we are well aware that the structures that determine mobility have and continue to be inherently unequal (Baynam, 2013; Canagarajah, 2017, 2020; Giddens, 2003). In addition to other traditional causes of migration such as economic collapse, natural disaster, war and transformations of sociopolitical systems (cf. Lutz, 2007), a scarcity of viable employment options in less developed nations often makes foreign salaries the only conceivable source of income for many of these nations' citizens and, thus, catalyzes external migration (Ladegaard, 2020; Lorente, 2017). According to Castles (2013: 122), a salient cause of movement and migration is 'growing inequality in incomes and human security between more and less developed countries'. It is precisely this population of economic migrants from less-developed countries that tends to encounter the largest number of constraints imposed by receiving nations (Codó, 2013; Gogia, 2006). Pre-pandemic, employers, like Magda in the US, one of the wealthiest nations worldwide, have profited from such mechanisms, which alleviate labor shortages and, when left unregulated, counteract the wage increases that normally accompany such shortages. At the same time, however, we are also aware that within many wealthier countries like the US and according to Magda herself, a viable workforce, especially within domestic work contexts, is lacking (Gonçalves & Schluter, 2020; Kaiper-Marquez & Makoni, 2022; Lorente, 2017; Romero, 2002; Romero et al., 2014). This phenomenon can sometimes result in increased competition and stagnant compensation for locals and their services. In this way, analysis of these dynamics highlights divides between the rich and the poor on global, national, regional and local scales.

The distinctiveness that characterizes Shine's domestic workers' migration experiences from Portugal, Central and South America also brings into focus the different degrees, speeds and shifts of existing social processes that are connected to diverse political, economic, social and cultural systems (Appadurai, 1996; Block, 2018; Blommaert, 2010; Coupland, 2010; Duchêne & Heller, 2012; Duchêne et al., 2013; Urry, 2007), which, in many ways, reflect existing asymmetries. For this reason, an analysis of the recent shifts in geographical flows as well as the mobility (and immobility) of Shine's migrant workers of certain linguistic and cultural backgrounds necessarily considers the regulation of specific markets as well as the ways in which political and economic control is maintained and perpetuated on the global stage through a wide range of neoliberal policies (Block, 2018; Canagarajah, 2016; Duchêne et al., 2013; Romero et al., 2014). Such considerations are shaped by histories of imperialism, nationalism, colonialism, capitalism and the globalized new economy (Gonçalves & Schluter, 2020; Heller & McElhinny, 2017; Kaiper-Marquez & Makoni, 2022), sites in which questions surrounding privilege, marginalization and inequality are intensified.

1.2.2 Previous studies on care and domestic work

In Section 1.2 we mentioned that female care/domestic workers are a (vulnerable) group of women that are largely under-represented within the new division of labor (Romero et al., 2014) and therefore, also unsurprisingly, also under-represented within academia and especially within the field of sociolinguistics. This is not to say of course that empirical studies have not been done. In fact, previous studies on care work and domestic labor in particular have often been theorized from a feminist perspective by analyzing the intersection of gender, race, ethnicity, class, sexuality and citizenship. Such studies find women's subordination to be a by-product of both capitalist and patriarchic structures, which, within a global economy, act to reinforce asymmetrical relations in often exploitive ways (Anderson, 2001; Chang, 2000; Hochschild, 2000; Lan, 2006; Lutz, 2011; Parreñas Salazar, 2011; Rollins, 1985; Romero *et al.*, 2014; Yeates, 2009). For Lutz (2011), domestic work, due to its highly feminine-gendered nature, plays *the* defining role in global, ethnic and gendered hierarchies and one which we often witnessed within our fieldwork at Shine with Magda, her female domestic workers and Shine's female customers. The studies mentioned above have been conducted largely within the fields of sociology and gender studies and have focused on various power dynamics of care/domestic work contexts, yet few (with the exception of Lan [2003]) have considered language as a key factor in the production and maintenance of inequality between female employers and their female employees.

Sociolinguistic studies addressing language learning, language use and, even, the commodification of language within domestic work contexts are in their relative infancy with the following work representing the bulk of the literature: Duff *et al.* (2000), Schwartz (2006), Lorente (2010, 2012, 2017), Ladegaard (2012, 2013, 2015, 2017, 2020), Dashti (2013), Divita (2014, 2020, 2021), Gonçalves (2015, 2021, 2022), Gonçalves and Schluter (2017, 2020), North (2017, 2018), Kaiper (2018), Ben Said (2019, 2022), Guinto (2019), Tang and Kan (2019), Vessey (2019), Chatterjee and Schluter (2020), Kaiper-Marquez and Makoni (2022), Borlongan (forthcoming), Vessey and Nicolai (2022), Rydell and Hannell (2022), Kaiper-Marquez (2022), Prinsloo (2022) and Rubdy and Pillai (2022). We have argued elsewhere (Gonçalves & Schluter, 2020) that such limited coverage is out of proportion, however, with the growing prominence of the global care/domestic work industry, which, owing to its transnational character, is increasingly pairing employers and/or customers together with workers who do not share a common linguistic or cultural background. The excerpt that appeared above in Extract (3) with Mrs Malloy and her non-English-speaking domestic worker represents one such example. Indeed, such scenarios are common within domestic labor contexts and Shine, in particular.

We contend that the underrepresentation of domestic workers globally is a complex process consisting of various key factors, which we have identified over the course of this project. We have outlined some of these in Figure 1.3.

These factors include domestic workers' vulnerable statuses, their places of work and residences as well as the ensuing methodological challenges that come with accessing individuals or groups of people that are not always readily visible (McDowell & Dyson, 2011). Additionally, when looking at vulnerable individuals, we also need to account for their personal trajectories and motivations for leaving their home countries.

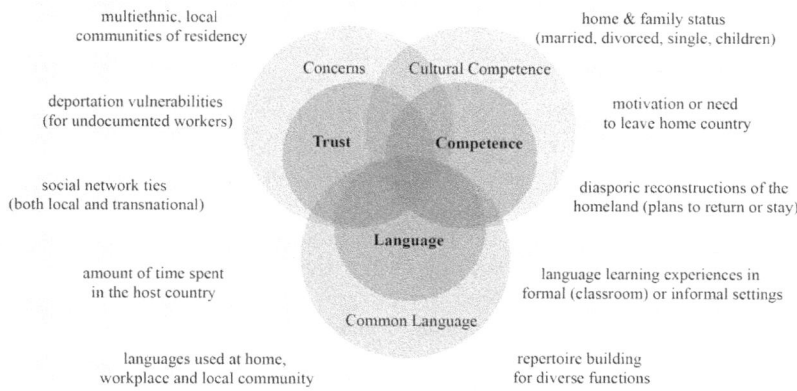

Figure 1.3 Key factors considered when working with Shine's migrant female domestic workers

Our figure is an adaptation from Blommaert's (2010) work, which we have tailored to our own study. We have also added the relevance of a common language, cultural competence and trust concerns that pertain to researchers and participants. Without factoring in these three points, our study would not have been feasible (for a thorough discussion of our methods and research design, see Chapter 2). Taken together, this may contribute to the dearth of related sociolinguistic scholarship on domestic labor and so-called 'blue-collar work' in general (see Gonçalves, 2020, for a thorough discussion). But perhaps it has to do with researchers' own networks and bourgeois agendas (Thurlow, 2020) or the fact that domestic labor is work performed backstage (Goffman, 1959), often in isolation (Strömmer, 2016) and thus not easily accessible.

Within the context of domestic labor, the home is the place where communication and the informal market economy meet. As a place, the home has historically not been considered to be a context worthy of academic study (Gonçalves, 2013; Gonçalves & Lanza, forthcoming; Piller, 2002), although within the subfields of Family Language Policy (Lanza, 2021; Van Mensel, 2020; Wright & Higgens, 2022) and Linguistic Landscapes (Gonçalves & Lanza, forthcoming; Melo-Pfeifer, 2022), this view of the home as a 'rich' fieldwork site is slowly changing. The home as a place of residence for employers and a workplace for domestic workers is commonly viewed as 'private' and thus beyond the purview of state regulation. This lack of state regulation, combined with transnational migrants' minority and marginalized standing (and thus citizenship status), frequently creates grounds for discrimination, exploitation, violence, abuse, harassment, forced labor and other dehumanizing practices among employers and their domestic workers (ILO, 2011, 2017; Ladegaard, 2017, 2020). As such, domestic workers are often found in 'hidden spaces' and not always voluntarily observable, making it difficult to access such individuals for research purposes.

The dire situation of many domestic workers globally was closely examined by the International Labor Organization at the Domestic Workers Convention No. 189 in 2011 in order to provide provisions and global standards to this group of workers. Nation-states were called upon to ensure that relevant national legislation applied to all workers in all work sectors in order for domestic workers to benefit from the same rights and protection as other workers. It must be noted here that the Convention and accompanying Domestic Workers Recommendation (2011: No. 201) are considered 'milestones' with respect to improving the working conditions of domestic workers worldwide with regard to working time, wages, social security, migration and labor inspections. This was a historical moment for domestic workers in that it was the first time that the International Labor Organization (ILO) had adopted international labor standards catered exclusively to this particular group of workers (ILO, 2013: 43). While specific policies and amendments in the law are desirable, these do not always lead to actual changes or an end to existing social inequalities, prejudices and discrimination (Gonçalves, 2022; Gonçalves & Schluter, 2020; Ladegaard, 2017; Lorente, 2017).

1.3 Domestic Labor in the US

In this section we narrow down our discussion of domestic labor within the context of the US. This is to provide readers with the relevant context of the situation in the US, where our study of Shine was carried out. According to the National Domestic Workers Alliance, there are well over 2.5 million domestic workers in the US (2020). More than 90% of these workers are women and disproportionately women of color and immigrants (Wolfe, 2020). Domestic workers in the US are considered to be low-wage workers and earn a median hourly wage of $10.21 compared to $17.55 for other workers (Wolfe, 2020). These low-level wages mean that many domestic workers on a national level are living in poverty (Wolfe, 2020). Most of these workers do not have social benefits, health insurance or paid leave; moreover, a large portion of them may have an insecure citizenship status. The combination of such socioeconomic factors makes this group of workers one of the most vulnerable to date. The Covid-19 pandemic also underscored the precarious nature of domestic work. Within the US alone, 94% of domestic workers reported that they received coronavirus-related cancellations by customers. Of those respondents, 70% were unsure if they would be rehired. The unpredictability for these workers, their jobs, their day-to-day finances and their economic survival carried psychological and emotional distress both nationally and worldwide (Cramer, 2020; Hubbard & Donovan, 2020; Jordan & Dickerson, 2020; Wang, 2021).

Domestic work is one of the oldest occupations to date. Prior to the Covid-19 pandemic domestic labor continued to experience growth despite predictions of its demise as a result of both industrialization and other modernization processes. The upsurge in middle-class women entering the workforce over the last few decades has contributed to the demand of domestic services (Anderson, 2001), where 'second shifts' (Hochschild, 1989), i.e. domestic work, continue to be outsourced. According to Gilder (1986), 'from 1890 to 1985 the participation in the work force of women between the ages of twenty-five and forty-four soared from 15 to 71 percent, with the pace of change tripling after 1950'. The shifts and changes of women in the labor force within particular sectors were also realized. Subsequent to World War II, women were entering professional domains that had previously and traditionally been occupied by men. Gilder claims that from '1972 to 1985 women's share of professional jobs increased from 44 to 49 percent and their share of "management" jobs nearly doubled, growing from 20 to 36 percent' (Hochschild, 1989). With women comprising nearly half of the US labor force, families with the economic means are able to hire domestic workers to cook, clean and/or look after their children. As we discuss in more detail in Chapter 3, Magda established Shine in the mid-1980s. This was precisely a point in time when historically more women were entering the workforce and due to what Magda felt was a 'gap in the market' on a regional and local level. Because of Magda's migrant and professional background, Magda was able to supply this demand by building a European-Portuguese-speaking-centric business regionally to serve a wealthy, mainly Anglophone customer base locally. The socioeconomic, racial and linguistic differences between Magda, her staff and customers are the topic of the next section.

1.4 Newark, Elizabeth and Westwood: Setting the Scene

1.4.1 Newark and Elizabeth: Working-class and culturally diverse neighborhoods

Shine's employees reside and spend much of their free time in the Portuguese ethnic enclaves of Newark and Elizabeth, New Jersey; they clean houses located in the upper-middle-class suburbs of Westwood, New Jersey and surrounding boroughs, which are located between 10 and 15 miles from both Newark and Elizabeth. A look at the participants' home and work environments provides a contrast between relative linguistic, racial and class homogeneity in the greater Westwood area as compared to the far more diverse urban contexts of Elizabeth and Newark.[1]

Due in large part to Shine's car pool service that transports workers between the Ironbound section of Newark and customers' houses, a number of Shine's employees reside in this neighborhood. At the time of our last fieldwork in 2015, Ironbound residents earned a median household income of $35,167 and were approximately 67.2% foreign-born.[2] This majority foreign-born demographic is reflected in residents' English language ability: the 'percentage of people that speak English not well or not at all' describes 43.4% of the Ironbound population.[3] In terms of race, 43.5% of the Ironbound's residents claimed to be 'non-Hispanic whites', 43.7% claim to be 'Hispanic' of all races, and 5.3% claimed to be 'black'.[4] Of the white population, many declared Portuguese origins. In fact, at 32.78% of the Ironbound's population, Portuguese represented the single largest ethnic community.[5]

The community's celebration of its Portuguese ties becomes apparent with a walk down Ferry Street, which is decorated in Portuguese national colors and flags and is referred to as *Portugal Avenue* (see Figures 1.4 and 1.5).

In an interview with the Director of Communications for the Ironbound Business District, (Gonçalves, 2012) finds this display of Portuguese identity to be authentic: local Portuguese residents reportedly own the majority of the Ironbound's commercial property. These owners are largely responsible for creating the Portuguese-centered semiotic landscape of the Ironbound District. The presence of Portuguese in this community has also recently attracted Brazilian migrants as well (Ramos-Zayas, 2012). The existence of a deeply rooted Portuguese-origin community with more recent arrivals from Brazil manifests itself

Figure 1.4 Portuguese flags decorating shops on Ferry Street

Figure 1.5 Ferry Street also known as Portugal Avenue

linguistically: European and Brazilian varieties of Portuguese are used to market many of the locally available goods and services.

In addition to its Lusophone inhabitants, the Ironbound District also has a growing Hispanophone population from South and Central America. As a result, different varieties of Spanish increasingly serve functions that are parallel to those of Portuguese in the community (see Figure 1.6).

Because a large percentage of the Ironbound population has limited English proficiency, English is generally not used as a common language between speakers from different L1 backgrounds. The resulting communication, instead, draws on a hybrid Portuguese-Spanish variety that relies on substantial negotiation and accommodation between interlocutors.

Elizabeth, New Jersey, home to some other Shine employees, also contains a mixture of Lusophone and Hispanophone inhabitants. For the purposes of the current discussion, we focused on the most up-to-date (2013) census figures from the two zip codes in which the Elizabeth-resident employees spend most of their time: 07201 and 07202. These two districts' median annual household income of $42,782 is slightly higher than that of the Ironbound District.[6] The top three racial classifications include 'Hispanic/Latino' (60.54%), 'non-Hispanic white' (18.34%) and black (17.5%). Of the white population, 54% claim either to have been born in Portugal (22.7%) or to be second-generation Americans of

Figure 1.6 Written varieties of Portuguese and Spanish on a shop window in the Ironbound

Portuguese descent (31.3%). This figure represents roughly 10% of the total population of these two areas.

Further demographic indicators suggest that, similar to the Ironbound District, English is not the most commonly spoken language in these zip codes: roughly 25% of the population speaks English at home. Given the considerable portion of inhabitants who were born in Portugal or have Portuguese parents, it is likely that Portuguese is this 'other Indo-European language' in a number of households. The importance of the Portuguese language and culture within these districts is reflected in the various eating establishments and community-gathering places that index Portuguese identity. Furthermore, the presence of services offered in Portuguese suggests that, similar to the Ironbound District, the size of the local Portuguese-dominant population is large enough to represent a market. The listing of Portuguese as the number one most commonly claimed ancestry of the US-born members of this population (5.75% of the total population) suggests that, although recent years have brought more Hispanophone residents to the area, there is a long-established history of Portuguese language and culture in these sections of Elizabeth, New Jersey.

In sum, these statistics suggest that, while Portuguese is one of the languages of the 07201 and 07202 zip codes of Elizabeth, Spanish is more dominant than in the Ironbound District. Similar to the Ironbound

District, however, is the low likelihood of English being spoken between the local residents, half of whom are foreign-born, and the likely reliance on more hybrid forms of communication between interlocutors with different languages.

1.4.2 Westwood: An elite upper-class suburb of New York City and location of Shine's headquarters

Shine employees commute daily from the ethnically diverse, Spanish-dominant and Portuguese-dominant, below-average-income communities in Elizabeth and Newark New Jersey to the company's headquarters located in the upper-class suburb of Westwood, New Jersey. From the company headquarters, they are then transported to their customers' houses, which are located in the greater Westwood area. This approximately 25-minute commute from Newark/Elizabeth to Westwood takes them to a setting in which the median house value is $707,093 and the median household income is $172,607 (according to 2017 data), which exceeds that of their home neighborhoods by roughly three times. Figures 1.7, 1.8, 1.9 and 1.10 are pictures of what average homes look like in the Ironbound and in Westwood, while Figures 1.11 and 1.12 indicate the kinds of shops (and many franchises like Gap Kids and Williams-Sonoma) found in downtown Westwood, which are indicative of a very different socioeconomic clientele.[7]

The demographic makeup of Westwood is unsurprisingly also quite different. According to 2010 census figures, the Westwood population consists of 84.5% White, 3.1% 'African American' and 5.6% Asian residents. At 4.9%, the percentage of Hispanic/Latino residents of all races in Westwood represents a fraction of the figures for the Ironbound (43.7%) and the 07201 and 07202 zip codes (60.54%).

Eighty-nine percent of Westwood residents were born in the United States. Unlike in the Ironbound and 07201 and 07202 zip codes, residents born in Portuguese- and Spanish-speaking countries are not common: Portugal is the birthplace of 3.1% of this 11% (0.034% of the total Westwood population) and, Brazil, 1.9% (0.021% of the total Westwood population). Colombia represents the most common Hispanophone country of origin (0.019% of the total population). This lower number of foreign-born residents, coupled with the relatively large percentage of non-native English speakers who claim high levels of proficiency in English (84%), contributes to a population that is far more English-dominant than those profiled in the Ironbound and Elizabeth. These figures highlight the absence of Portuguese and Spanish in the Westwood area. Furthermore, in our interviews with customers, which took place entirely in English, we were able to confirm residents' low/non-existent competence in Spanish and Portuguese in addition to their English-language dominance. Given the complex multilingual situation in these areas, we now turn to a

Figures 1.7 and 1.8 Pictures of homes in the Ironbound neighborhood

Figures 1.9 and 1.10 Pictures of homes in Westwood

18 Domestic Workers Talk

Figure 1.11 Gap Kids in downtown Westwood

Figure 1.12 Williams-Sonoma in downtown Westwood

broader discussion of multilingualism in the US while incorporating our own observations from Shine.

1.5 Multilingual Communities, a Multilingual Company and Power

Previous literature within sociolinguistics, linguistic anthropology and multilingual studies have indicated the existence of hierarchical ordering of languages within multilingual communities and settings (cf. De Swaan, 2001; Gumperz, 1982; Piller, 2017). Studies conducted in such contexts have shown that speakers of different language varieties within a defined space and time are often considered to be of unequal status. While earlier studies have often aligned with a Bourdieusian perspective where the dominant language is usually the language associated with authority and, in the vast majority of cases, also the state (Bourdieu, 1991), more contemporary work questions the ideas of power, authority and domination with regard to different language speakers, their value and the status of languages (and their users) in different multilingual contexts (Gonçalves, 2020a; Kramsch, 2021; Serwe, 2021). This is certainly the case where more recent scholarship is looking beyond 'just language' to understand how multimodality and embodiment are key factors in comprehending the complexity of communication within multilingual settings (Bucholtz & Hall, 2016; Canagarajah, 2020; Gonçalves, 2020a; Hua & Li, 2022; Kusters *et al.*, 2017; Otsuji & Pennycook, 2015; Schluter, 2020; Theodoropoulou, 2020) and a key theoretical perspective which drives our analysis in Chapter 5.

In our earlier work about Magda's role as Shine's main language broker and thus linguistic authority (Gonçalves & Schluter, 2017), we found instances of what Grillo (1989) terms 'legitimated domination' of Magda over her migrant employees. Drawing on Weber's (1958) work, Grillo (1989) understands authority as 'legitimated domination', which is similar to Bourdieu's vision of symbolic power as 'invisible' in its practitioners' ability to exercise power without actually exerting force. Magda's ability to control communication at different levels within Shine was a salient example of how both overt and covert power works among herself and her staff (company internal communication) and between herself and her customers (company external communication) in the linguistic management of Shine. In these ways, we found that Shine's employees as minority language-speaking migrants are often the experiencers of legitimated domination due to their subordinate social, cultural, economic, political and linguistic statuses within the local, regional and national context of the receiving society (Goldstein, 1997; Grillo, 1989).

On a national scale, this subordinate status applies to the historical dominance of English over such migrant languages as Portuguese in the US despite the country's unexamined multilingual past (Crawford, 1992) and long tradition of widespread cultural and linguistic pluralism (cf. Fuller & Leeman, 2020; Potowski, 2010). Portuguese, the primary migrant language of focus in our study, ranks 11th among the most widespread non-English languages spoken in the US. These speakers number approximately 687,126, which accounts for 0.24 % of the national population (Carvahlo, 2010: 223). The number of Portuguese speakers within the state of New Jersey has grown in the past decades (Carvahlo, 2010; Scott, 2009), especially in Elizabeth and the Ironbound District of Newark, or 'Latino Newark' (Ramos-Zayas, 2012).

In these ways, the statistics of Portuguese speakers point to a clear reorientation of power when it comes to Portuguese minority language speakers on national, regional and local scales. European Portuguese is the dominant and most powerful language regionally within these neighborhoods and locally within Shine.

Indeed, language functions as a symbolic, interactional, material and ideological resource. On the one hand, it can perpetuate inequality by facilitating modes of domination and subordination between individuals of different status like Magda, her customers and Shine employees. On the other hand, those with access to linguistic and other semiotic resources may exploit them for their own empowerment as we witnessed with Magda and her employees and between employees themselves. These considerations are relevant to every communicative context; however, they are particularly salient to workplace settings (Moyer, 2018). We argue that these considerations are further accentuated in domestic work contexts, which function as prime sites of both privilege and marginalization. Within these sites, extremely asymmetrical power relations stem from unequal access to economic, material, linguistic and social capital (Bourdieu, 1991) and, in some cases, also citizenship rights.

Within the current study, participants' undocumented status, low education levels and limited English proficiency represent the most salient factors that restrict their access to the marketplace and account for the subordinate position in society. Magda's American citizenship, university-level education, English-language proficiency and position as Shine's founder grant her a higher status among her employees. As the company founder and boss, Magda would still have more power than her employees even without these different forms of capital. A full discussion of these influences on Shine and the role of different languages and varied repertoires will be explored in the following chapters.

1.6 Overview of Chapters

In Chapter 2 entitled *Advancing Methodology*, we discuss the mixed methodological approach employed in this ethnography, which contributes to studies in sociolinguistics and multilingual studies. The chapter begins with a vignette by Kellie explaining a vivid memory she had as a teenager when she was with Magda. The methodological advantages and disadvantages of conducting a study with a close family member are also discussed as are the qualitative research methods we employed, which include critical, post-critical and mobile ethnography.

In Chapter 2, we also present the various data sets collected for this study over a 10-year time span, which include participant observation and field notes, interviews, Shine's company pamphlet and a survey conducted with Shine customers. The analytical frameworks used to analyze our data sets consisted of both discourse and content analysis. Indeed, our mixed methodological approach allowed us to triangulate our diverse data sets enabling us to get a more accurate and richer description of the linguistic and semiotic practices undertaken within Shine.

In Chapter 3, we shift our focus to Magda, Shine's owner, and investigate her personal and professional trajectory as well as the components of emotional intelligence, which until now has not been considered within language and workplace studies within sociolinguistics. In this chapter, we analyze Magda's no-nonsense business leadership style, as well as exploring Magda's 'softer side' through our discussion of emotional intelligence. We discuss and illustrate with examples how the various components of emotional intelligence according to Goleman (2000, 2015), which consist of *self-awareness*, *self-regulation*, *motivation*, *empathy* and *social skills*, pertain to Magda. We argue that Magda's high level of emotional intelligence, which she has acquired throughout her life, contributes to her dynamic leadership style within Shine. Chapter 3 also illuminates Magda's multifaceted identities as a female, migrant business owner by tracing both her personal and professional trajectories as a transnational migrant and successful entrepreneur. These insights provide readers with a deeper and more nuanced picture of Magda and show how her life circumstances and certain choices paved the way to establish a small private successful business.

Chapter 4 focuses on neoliberal capital flows, migration and belonging where Shine's migrant employees' orientations are intricately tied to the three primary tenets of investment including capital, identity and ideology. In this chapter, we look at the choices and reasons behind Shine's Hispanophone Latino workers, who could potentially seek employment at one of the numerous Hispanophone-dominant cleaning companies in the greater Newark area. The chapter explores the different mechanisms that make such choices viable options for some of Shine's employees. As such, the chapter discusses different theoretical concepts such as *horizontal assimilation* and *decapitalization* as they pertain to individuals and particular varieties with respect to their assessment and valuation. Horizontal assimilation is the act of strongly affiliating with the culture of a non-dominant group that is different from one's own (Prashad, 2001). *Decapitalization* (Martín Rojo, 2013; Moyer, 2018) is the process through which linguistic capital diminishes as a result of a shift in a language's status from dominant to minority, which is most certainly the case with European Portuguese within the larger setting of New Jersey, but less applicable to Shine's context. As such, the analysis in Chapter 4 addresses the extent to which the notion of decapitalization applies to Portuguese as a migrant language in the Newark area among Shine employees and more specifically, three of the company's four Hispanophone employees.

Chapter 5 explores Post-Humanist applied linguistics and embodied communication with a focus on the ways in which Lusophone domestic workers communicate with their Anglophone customers. Since many of these domestic workers and customers do not share a common language, we investigate the skillful deployment of resources between these individuals in order for communication to be achieved. The chapter highlights the recent focus within the field of sociolinguistics on embodied communication (Bucholtz & Hall, 2016), semiotic repertoires (Gonçalves, 2020a; Kusters, 2021; Kusters *et al.*, 2017) and Post-Humanist applied linguistics (Pennycook, 2018). We discuss how investment in English becomes secondary to the establishment of mutual understanding. We explain how our findings are grounded in the specific Shine workplace context and where additional research is required to understand their alignment with larger trends. At the same time, our findings could serve as a basis for similar studies to be carried out in different workplaces across various cultural settings to address the distinction between communication and language in addition to the level of influence of dominant-language ideologies.

Chapter 6 provides a summary of this book, our findings, our shortcomings and future directions. We discuss what remains to be done in the future within language and workplace studies within multilingual blue-collar contexts. We emphasize the need to look beyond the use of complex language practices only and also consider the resources individuals can deploy in order for communication to be achieved. It is also in this chapter that we reassess the notion of value as it pertains to languages and English in particular within this local workplace context. Finally, we provide readers with an up-to-date summary of Shine since the pandemic and Magda's retirement, outlining some of the new challenges domestic workers face within precarious employment. These challenges are not always related to communication, but they are influenced and exacerbated by socioeconomic and sociopolitical processes taking place on different scales at a precise moment in time. As researchers and ethnographers, we have learned a lot from Shine and underscore how our findings have helped to advance our understanding of communication in migrant domestic workplace settings with respect to researcher positionality, language policy, language brokering, migrant entrepreneurship, diasporic affiliations, accommodation, multicompetence and embodiment. We hope our work will inspire others to venture out into 'hidden domains' that shed light on salient processes of language and communication to exemplify just how complex multilingual matters are.

Notes

(1) The data presented here come from census figures, which provide a picture of the highlighted areas' demographics with the caveat that they tend to underrepresent the Hispanophone and Lusophone residents because they exclude those who are undocumented.
(2) This statistic comes from http://zipatlas.com/us/nj/newark/zip-07105.htm#income (Accessed on 27 June, 2016)
(3) These data come from http://www.city-data.com/neighborhood/North-Ironbound-Newark-NJ.html (Accessed on 27 June, 2016)
(4) These figures come from http://statisticalatlas.com/neighborhood/New-Jersey/Newark/North-Ironbound/Race-and-Ethnicity (Accessed on 27 June, 2016). Because of some of the residents' undocumented status, many of whom are from Central and South America, we acknowledge that the percentage of the population that the census counts as 'Hispanic' is, most likely, lower than the actual figures.
(5) http://zipatlas.com/us/nj/newark/zip-07105.htm#demographics (Accessed on 27 June, 2016).
(6) Statistics for this description have been calculated according to the information found on both http://www.city-data.com/zips/07201.html and http://www.city-data.com/zips/07202.html (Accessed on 28 June, 2016).
(7) These images are meant to be illustrative only. An account of the linguistic/semiotic landscape of all neighborhoods is beyond the scope of this book. For an account of the semiotic landscape of the Ironbound neighborhood, cf. Gonçalves (2012).

2 Advancing Methodology: Using a Mixed Methodological Approach within a Multilingual Cleaning Company

2.1 Introduction

Readers know by now that Magda, the company owner of Shine, is a family member of Kellie's whom she has known her entire life. In fact, when Magda began her business in the mid-1980s, after a career in finance, several family members assisted in circulating Shine flyers throughout different neighborhoods in the town where Magda resided. Kellie was one of those family members and at the time just seven years old.

Kellie spent a lot of time with Magda as a child, especially at her home, which also serves as Shine's headquarters. Magda had set up an office in her furnished basement, which is still there today. On occasions when Magda had to meet a customer or monitor a cleaning lady, Kellie often accompanied her and witnessed first-hand how she managed her company. At first, Kellie didn't have much of a choice in escorting Magda on these business outings, but as she got older and could be left unattended, she often went along with Magda voluntarily out of general interest and curiosity and, later, pure fascination. Magda has been and continues to be a savvy business owner who controls all aspects of Shine even right down to the micro-management of her employees and clients' communication (Gonçalves & Schluter, 2017). She is no-nonsense yet is extremely personable with both her staff and her customers. Magda's experience within the financial sector for nearly a decade has given her an enormous advantage in terms of navigating the supply and demand sides of a local and regional cleaning business while managing individuals of different cultural, linguistic, socioeconomic backgrounds and legal statuses (see Chapter 3 for a thorough discussion). For Kellie, Magda's appeal as a business owner and entrepreneur was managing a staff of 20–30 people, most of whom were migrant women from Portugal, Brazil and Central America with varying competency levels in English and a majority Anglophone customer base of nearly 300 people, who resided in upper-class suburbs of New York City. We claim that Magda's main assets as a businesswoman and leader are her emotional intelligence, intercultural communication skills, financial competence, high professional standards and attention to detail when it comes to both her customers and employees. While Magda is at once very empathetic toward her customers and employees, she also stands firmly behind well-defined principles that guide her explicit rebukes of their behaviors she will not tolerate. What follows is a case in point.

2.2 A Vignette by Kellie: My Memory of Magda as a Teenager

I vividly remember one particular scenario in which I went with Magda to a potential customer's house, a visit scheduled in order to inspect it and give the potential customer an estimate about the first cleaning job as well as set the price for this house if the customer was willing to accept Magda's offer. Magda made it very clear to all potential customers that she first needed to inspect the house and walk around it, enabling her to set prices since each house was a different size and required specific instructions based on the customer's needs, but also due to valuable items in the house such as antique furniture and rugs.

When we walked into the house, a man greeted us. This occasion was rather rare: most of Magda's interactions with customers were done with the women of the home. This resonates with findings of other studies, where women are considered to stereotypically be responsible for managing the feminine-gendered nature of domestic work (Gonçalves & Schluter, 2020; Hochschild, 1989; Lorente, 2017; Lutz, 2011; Romero et al., 2014). In this particular scenario, the woman was working and had arranged for her husband to be present during the initial meeting. As usual, Magda got out her pen and pad and started to walk around the house. She asked the homeowner questions and took extensive notes on his answers, the condition of the house and its residents. Magda asked about the furniture, the rugs, the presence of pets and children, but she also inquired about the customer's needs. What kind of cleaning would he like to be done? Did he envision a weekly, bi-weekly or monthly service, for example? All of these questions came to the fore during this initial visit. Magda explained that the first cleaning job was pricey as several of her cleaning staff would be there and devote an entire day to cleaning the house, including all walls, ceilings, woodwork and windows in order to get it to a standard which they would be able to maintain on a weekly or bi-weekly basis. Magda was not in favor of cleaning houses on a monthly basis as this often entailed much more work for her and her staff; therefore, she only provided this service in very exceptional circumstances.

After the inspection, Magda set the initial cleaning fee at $600.00. The man was shocked and, quite frankly, so was I. I think our strong reaction accounts for its firm grounding in my memory. The man informed her that this price was too expensive and that he would have to consult with his wife before making any decisions, but that he had envisioned and hoped for a much lower fee. Magda stated that in order for the house to be cleaned properly, a lot of work needed to be done. She reiterated the heavy workload involved, including the three to four cleaners needed to be there from 8am to 5pm and Magda's intense monitoring of their progress several times throughout the day in order to ensure that it was 'immaculate'. Magda stated that of course she understood his financial concern and need to discuss Shine's services and prices with his wife, but that he also needed to keep in mind that the service her company was providing was an outstanding one, which was professional, insured and bonded.

When Magda and I got back into her car, I remember telling her quite honestly, that $600.00 was a lot of money, and she responded, 'Yes, I know, I don't want to do this house'. This was my first informal class regarding the fundamental concepts of economics and an introduction to the supply and demand relationships within a market economy. I was 14. Magda then explained to me that she had intentionally set a high fee for the initial cleaning with the hope that the potential client would actually decline the offer. Magda was not interested in providing her services in this house because the house was a difficult one to clean for a number of reasons. First, she had already calculated what she could charge him on either a weekly or even bi-weekly basis but maintained that it would not be profitable to her as a business owner because the house would always require two cleaners rather than one; therefore, it would not cover her expenditures. Secondly, she did not want to subject her employees to such a difficult cleaning job. As a result, the price set by Magda was one she knew was too high, but it also reflected the current demand within this particular niche market. If the client had accepted the initial cleaning fee set at $600.00, then it would be financially profitable for Magda's business. It would also demonstrate the shortage of supply of competent, locally available house cleaners.

In the end, the potential client did not request Shine's services due to the high fee. After all, this was about business. In economic terms, the demand and notion of customer choice come to the fore and perhaps exemplify what Massey in 'Vocabularies of the Economy' (2013: 3) would claim to be 'a specific activity and relationship erased by a general relationship of buying and selling that is given precedence over it'. In line with economic theory, customers, consumers and clients 'whose prime duty (and source of power and pleasure) is to make choices' (2013: 4). Magda's offer allows customers to make the choice of accepting or foregoing her services despite knowing that 99% of the time, most customers *will decline the offer. In many ways, this kind of verbal transaction allows Magda to maintain a professional stance toward her customer base by never refusing to take on a customer and their house, but allows the customers to make the final decision or at least give them the impression that they have.*

This vignette highlights several points about ethnography, a qualitative research method considered to be one of the most challenging but also the most rewarding (Gonçalves, 2020; Levon, 2018). First, it accounts for the historical aspect of the project. Second, it reflects the relevance of ethnography in different phases, consisting of an exploratory phase, a strategic phase and a systematic phase. Third, it situates the study as a moral practice, one that is both political and personal. Fourth, it underscores research as reflexive, where the positionality of the researcher (whether an insider or an outsider) is never neutral. And lastly, it highlights the saliency of methodological access to a particular group of people.

2.3 Research Design: Exploratory and Systematic Phases of Our Study

Although the above vignette is just one example that shows the ways in which Magda managed her business with customers and her selection of them – rather than the other way around – as a result of the high demand for her company's services, Kellie was not sure about exposing it. The workings of Magda's business and Kellie's long-standing personal relationships with both Magda and several of her employees made the decision to carry out this research project one which was ethically, personally and, in many ways, also politically challenging. In spite of the challenges, the decision to finally carry out this project was a joint one made among Magda, her employees, her customers, Kellie and Anne. As academics, we both have several research interests in common as well as complementary language skills. In our opinion, these complementary backgrounds added balance to our perspective of Shine. Because of Kellie's close familial relationship with Magda, Anne's insight as an 'outsider' increased the reliability of this study's overall research design, data collection and ensuing analysis.

According to Johnstone (2000: 90), 'ethnographic research almost always occurs in two phases, one relatively unplanned and exploratory, the second more systematic'. We 'officially' began this ethnographic study in 2011 when we received permission from Magda to investigate the communicative practices within her business. However, observations of Magda and the communication done within Shine unofficially began three decades ago as previously mentioned. As researchers committed to post-critical ethnography, we are compelled to be reflexive and honest about access, relationships, methods and challenges while simultaneously protecting the anonymity of our research participants. In doing so, we have also faced several ethical, moral, political and personal questions, which have made the decision to carry out such a study at times even more challenging. In her work on qualitative research methods, Mason (2002: 4) states that:

> qualitative research requires a highly active engagement from its practitioners. Indeed, any researcher must identify and resolve a whole range of issues in the research process, most of which are specific in some way to their particular research project, and many of which cannot be anticipated in advance.

This was indeed the case with our study that investigates language practices within a multilingual cleaning company and a business that employs undocumented transnational female migrant workers, a population that is particularly vulnerable.

Within Shine, we knew many of the employees and the employer, and were also aware that their participation in our study could be seen as a type of exploitation or 'goodwill' resonating with Cameron's work. According to Cameron (2001: 22),

> the people we are closest to are often, ironically, the people we feel least compunction about exploiting – or perhaps we do not see it as exploitation, since we are confident of their goodwill towards us and their desire to help us.

A few studies within sociolinguistics and sociology have illustrated that concealment usually incurs negative consequences (i.e. Coates' 1996 study on deceiving her close friends). This finding has also emerged within a domestic labor context: Rollins (1985) engaged in what she called 'deliberate deception' in working as a domestic worker to gain access to employers. She states:

> The guilt came from my comprised sense of fair play (and that is why it was stronger in relation to more humane women than in relation to the more exploitive). But the deeper unease came from what I thought my actions might do to me as well as from what I was doing to others, and from my concern about the long-term ramifications of the systematic use of deception for a discipline and for a society that so easily objectifies human beings. For to dehumanize others is to dehumanize oneself; to treat others as objects is to make oneself more of an object. Something of my human spirit, however minute a something, would be lost, compromised in the process. The immediate question became: is what can be gained worth the loss? I decided it was.

For Rollins, pretending to be a domestic worker and working as one rather than being honest about her role as a sociological researcher may be considered unethical. Rollins' interpretation of the 'Code of Ethics' established by the American Sociological Association was that subjects must not be exposed to substantial risk or personal harm, and, where those may occur, informed consent is required.

A lot has changed regarding ethics approval and securing informed consent within the social sciences since Rollins carried out her study in the early 1980s. While we made our research aims and agenda very explicit to Magda, her employees and Shine customers, Kellie had conflicting feelings about investigating Magda's company for several reasons. First, Kellie did not want to exploit Magda, her customers and, most importantly, her employees, four of whom were undocumented workers and, therefore, also vulnerable participants. Kellie had spoken at length several times to Magda about engaging in a study of this kind, which Magda was very open to. She even thought it might be good for her business. However, Kellie also knew that such an investigation could have potential consequences for Magda as a business owner as well as for her employees. Most of all, it could have ramifications for the long-term familial relationship between Kellie and Magda in addition to the personal relationships between Kellie and Magda's employees, which Kellie did not want to jeopardize for the purposes of research. In fact, most of Magda's employees knew Kellie, some better than others. Many of Magda's employees, especially those who had been working for Magda since the establishment of her company, had known Kellie for over 20 years. When Kellie was a teenager, Magda often consulted her about written correspondence with customers, for example, checking memos, notes and the company booklet intended for customers. During university holidays one summer, Kellie also worked for Magda as a driver, transferring employees from different houses when key cleaning staff and drivers were out of the country on holiday. In these ways, Kellie was not just a family member of Magda's but also one of her former employees. As such, there are both advantages and challenges to carrying out such a study, which we have outlined in Table 2.1.

On the one hand, and like any ethnographic study, as a researcher, 'one is entering into a specific kind of conversation, one in which you have to make **explicit** your assumptions, expectations, commitments, argumentation procedures and all your other ways of working' (Heller *et al*., 2018: 25, bold in the original). On the other hand, we also felt very strongly about bringing this study into the open not only to shed light on informal and ethnic economies of a domestic labor and blue-collar work context, but also to investigate a private business in the US in which Portuguese – rather than English – is the company-internal language. In it, Portuguese is required by workers for socioeconomic mobility. When we brought up the topic of English competence among Magda's employees, for example, she told us the following:

Table 2.1 Methodological advantages and challenges of embarking on this kind of study

Advantages	Challenges
Access to a private business and key informants	Being 'too close' to the research site and context; risk of exposing the business
Familiarity with most individuals at Shine, especially Magda and respecting our mutual trust	Exploiting individuals; jeopardizing personal relationships for the sake of research
Consent from Magda, employees and clients relatively quickly	Navigating consent with the understanding that many of the employees' consent resulted from our relationship with Magda, who holds power over them
Have unfettered access to different data types, i.e. emails, texts, notes and company booklet	Being explicit about how we would use and analyze data, obtain permission for publications
Contribute to different academic fields and also to Shine	Being able to handle guilty feelings associated with the potential to fracture relationships
The valuing of participants' opinions, which, in turn, helped them to view their experience and perspective as meaningful	Handling vulnerable individuals (especially undocumented ones) and being culturally sensitive to their needs and requests

Extract (1)

1. Magda: Mrs Smith called me, she was just curious, for example, Maria worked for me for 21
2. years and retired, she said, 'How long has Maria lived in the US @@' and I said, 'Oh, you
3. know, since 1974' but she spoke absolutely not a word of English and I just explained to Mrs
4. Smith, 'You know, Maria lived in a Portuguese community, where, you know, she comes home
5. her husband speaks Portuguese, the, the erm, the grown-up sons already and erm, you know,
6. she goes to the supermarket, it's Portuguese, and if she goes to buy a piece of...erm...an outfit
7. you know? Ferry Street it's like a little Portugal' so erm

The fact that several of Magda's employees had resided in the US for well over 20 years and had managed to support themselves without speaking any English at all was a theme we wanted to explore in detail. In other words, much like Goldstein's (1997) seminal work in Ontario, Canada, we also wanted to test the assumption that English is the language needed and used within an English-dominant local context and linked to socio-economic mobility. Like Rollins, but without engaging in 'deliberate deception', we asked ourselves, is what can be gained worth the loss? After much deliberation and many discussions, we too decided that it was. At the same time, we also tried to mitigate all potential losses.

2.4 Data: Data Collection and Data Triangulation

In 2011, we obtained permission from Magda to begin collecting data. Magda facilitated participant recruitment and interview scheduling by discussing the study with her staff and obtaining participant permission from them. Similarly, Magda sent out a one-page description of the study and invitation to participate to all of her customers via email. Having Magda do the initial introduction to our study with both her employees and customers meant that they were already familiar with our research objectives. Moreover, we were presented to Magda's staff and clients as a family member and 'a friend of a friend' (Gonçalves, 2013; Milroy, 1980). This allowed participants to relax and open up during interviews.

In our first round of data collection in 2011, we conducted 41 informal, open-ended interviews (16–90 minutes in length), which were recorded and transcribed. During this interview period, we also took field notes and shadowed Magda's workday for several hours at a time over a seven-day period. In these ways, we were able to observe her management, leadership and organizational style (Holmes *et al.*, 2011; Rutherford, 2001; Sinek, 2014). It also allowed us to view her brokering duties first-hand as well as ask any follow-up questions.

Through our relationship with Magda, we also gained access to written material of her company, including an information booklet intended for customers as well as copies of memos given to her staff. Our relatively unfettered access to both participants and related materials sets our study apart from the majority that explore these topics through similar methodological approaches (Ben Said, 2019; Lorente, 2017; see also Gonçalves & Schluter, 2020, and Kaiper-Marquez & Makoni, 2022). Due to budget sizes, time restrictions and difficulties obtaining participants' consent, many such ethnographic studies become accounts or situated, discursive performances (cf. Briggs, 1986; Ladegaard, 2017) about participants' description of their language and behavior with limited potential for triangulation. Data triangulation was achieved in our own study by consulting with Magda, her employees and customers about language claims, language use and management style. These findings subsequently underwent additional triangulation through our own participant observation, field notes and follow-up interviews.

Both authors grew up in New Jersey and are multilingual speakers of English, Portuguese and Spanish (Spanish with various proficiency levels). This background facilitated data collection procedures, especially in terms of speech elicitation from all participants. The authors' ties to New Jersey provided another advantage: follow-up interviews with Magda, her employees and customers which could be conducted during trips back home. In 2015, we engaged in another round of data collection with Magda and a handful of her employees. Since 2011, we have been in regular contact with Magda through different modes, i.e. face-to-face interaction, telephone calls, Skype chats and text messaging in order to monitor developments at Shine.

2.5 Poststructuralist Perspectives and Epistemological Shifts within Sociolinguistics: Employing Mobile, Critical and Post-Critical Ethnography

This book is highly influenced by poststructuralist perspectives and a broader epistemological shift that accounts for critical and ethnographical approaches within the field of sociolinguistics. In line with 'critical-constructivist sociolinguistics', we understand language as a 'social practice with speakers drawing on all kinds of linguistic resources for their own purposes' (Bell, 2014: 9), which include specific communicative practices, repertoires, 'bits of language' (Blommaert, 2010) as well as – and often in conjunction with – other semiotic means and artifacts (Gonçalves, 2020a; Otsuji & Pennycook, 2015; Theodoropoulou, 2020). In these ways, our work aligns with the recent paradigm shift in sociolinguistics, where the deployment of semiotic resources, of which one is language, allows for a fuller understanding of communicative practices in different contexts that are characterized by multiple mobilities at a specific, spacio-temperal, historical moment.

It is not surprising, therefore, that when epistemological shifts take place, and old paradigms are being reconsidered, our methodological approaches be questioned and tailored accordingly. Such considerations embed our work within contemporary sociocultural and political changes and challenges. This does not mean, however, that former accounts must be dismissed altogether. Instead, they should be viewed in tandem with pre-existing approaches that have and continue to work well for social scientists. For these reasons and based on the context of our study, we draw on mobile ethnography, critical ethnography and post-critical ethnography.

For many scholars in the social sciences, ethnography – and perhaps most recently, critical ethnography – has become the preferred research method. This may be due to critical ethnography's focus on social change especially at a time that is significantly marked by a heightened sense of instability, unpredictability and inequality for many individuals, especially those located at the lower end of the socioeconomic scale. The field of sociolinguistics has been concerned with public engagement, the social implications of research findings and giving back to the research community (Cameron *et al.*, 1992; Gonçalves, 2020b; Levon, 2018; Rickford, 1999; Wolfram, 1993, to name a few).

Most recently, many scholars working with vulnerable and marginalized groups of people have taken their research findings and called for social justice through active sociopolitical action. We see this in Barrett's

(2016: iii) call for scholars to engage in work that foregrounds 'active, intercultural democratic citizenship' and in the work of Lim *et al.* (2018) with regard to 'linguistic citizenship'. Chomsky, in his well-known work titled, 'The Responsibility of Intellectuals' (1967; Allott *et al.*, 2019) discusses the privileged positions of intellectuals and their responsibility to be frank and speak out on others' behalf. We are well aware that the findings and discussions presented in this book may be read by students, fellow researchers, Magda and perhaps several of Shine's customers and even employees, but to what extent do our findings reach a wider audience, like business owners or even policymakers? Is striving for social justice as Pennycook (2022: 15) states 'an ideal goal rather than a serious program for social change'? We have asked ourselves, what are we actually changing and for whom? Indeed, some researchers claim that if change is accomplished on a very small scale, i.e. that of the researcher's perspective through engagement of researcher projects, then this already classifies as change on the societal level (Cambell & Lassiter, 2015). More recently, however, Ladegaard and Phipps (2020: 72) call for 'a renewed commitment to our joint role as scholars and public, transformative intellectuals' by translating our research findings into social action. While the latter is indeed difficult to achieve and is often constrained by a number of factors, one aim of this book is to shed light on a vulnerable group of individuals, all of whom are migrant women, in order for 'their voices' to be heard, keeping in mind that those voices are our own intersubjective representations of them.

Working with this group of individuals was not always easy. As researchers, we had to be extremely flexible with our participants and, despite our project planning and research design, this project often deviated in ways we could not foresee. For example, we were not able to speak to as many Shine customers as we had originally planned as many were on vacation during our summer fieldwork trips. In another instance, one domestic worker did not want to conduct a follow-up interview with us as she had just experienced a loss in her family abroad and was not in the mood to talk to us, which we understood and respected. As such, this project has resulted in a very data-driven study. Data-driven studies are those in which 'empirical methodologies become the foundation for inquiry' (Madison, 2012: 5). The methodologies employed in this project consist of carrying out 'multi-sited ethnography' (Marcus, 1995; Martin-Jones & Martin, 2017; Pietikäinen *et al.*, 2016), 'mobile ethnography' (Gonçalves, 2020b; Novoa, 2015; Sheller & Urry, 2006) critical ethnography (Heller *et al.*, 2018; Madison, 2012; Martin-Jones & Martin, 2017; Thomas, 1992) and post-critical ethnography (Lester & Anders, 2018; Noblit *et al.*, 2004). These various modes of ethnography allowed for a range of observation and recording techniques that we have been observing for years unofficially and, since 2011, officially, as listed in Table 2.2.

Table 2.2 Mixed methods and data sets used in this study

Research methods	Observing the settings and people's movement within them	Survey	Written material	Examing conversations
Data	Participant observation in and outside of work; Shadowing Fieldnotes	Survey conducted with 30 customers about language practices with Shine employees	Examined company pamphlet, emails, notes and texts to customers Examined notes and texts to employees	Carried out over 50 interviews with participants Resulted in a multilingual corpus of approximately 300,000 words
Analytical framework	Content analysis	Content analysis	Content and discourse analysis	Discourse analysis

As stated in Section 2.4 above, the mixed methodological approaches used in this study allowed for the cross-checking of different sources, which facilitated data triangulation. Data triangulation therefore allowed us to get a more accurate and richer description of the language practices within Shine, broadening our understanding of how diverse individuals and groups interact with one another at different levels. This was especially relevant since what people think they do, and what they claim to do, does not always correspond to what they actually do (Verschueren, 1979). The diverse methods used in this study also share epistemological assumptions about how to approach the social world empirically. While content analysis allowed us to examine themes that emerged within different text types (such as our field notes, the company booklet, survey, notes and texts), discourse analysis (Johnstone, 2002) allowed us to analyze language in a very explicit and systematic way by focusing on aspects of both structure and function. In the following sections, we discuss the key ethnographic approaches used in this study, beginning with mobile ethnography.

2.6 Mobile Ethnography: A Case of Co-Present Immersion and Sustained Engagement with Participants

Mobile ethnography is not a new methodology within the social sciences: it has existed since the 19th century with the work of (cultural) anthropologists moving around in their field of study, living together, and observing their informants' behavior and sociocultural practices (cf. Mead, 1928, 1930). The work of Marcus (1995) is especially relevant here since it sparked a debate within the social sciences about how to conduct fieldwork, advocating that methodological changes were required in order to properly observe and document particular social phenomena across diverse spaces extending beyond a single site. The sentiments of Marcus's work could not ring more true for the diversity and mobility captured by contemporary postmodern times (Giddens, 2003). In a more recent paper, O'Reilly (2009: 144) claims that 'in the context of increased global interconnectivity, and mobility of people, objects and ideas, ethnographers are taking their methodology to multiple and mobile places and spaces'. Indeed, the rise and popularity of the mobilities paradigm within contemporary social science have been brought to light by the work of John Urry and many others. In 2004, Law and Urry stated that methods within the social sciences do not deal well with:

> the fleeting – that which is here today and gone tomorrow, only to reappear again the day after tomorrow. They deal poorly with the distributed – that is to be found here and there but not in between – or that which slips and slides between one place and another. They deal poorly with the multiple – that which takes different shapes in different places. They deal poorly with the non-causal, the chaotic, the complex. And such methods have difficulty dealing with the sensory – that which is subject to vision, sound, taste, smell; with the emotional – time-space compressed outbursts of anger, pain, rage, pleasure, desire, or the spiritual; and the kinaesthetic – the pleasures and pains which follow the movement and displacement of people, objects, information and ideas. (2004: 403–404)

For us, it was clear. We wanted to deal with the fleeting, the multiple, the complex, the sensory and the emotional. As such, we needed to do a lot more than observe and talk with our participants. Engaging in mobile methods involves 'walking with', or traveling with, people as a form of sustained engagement. It is, thus, regarded as 'first-hand social science' (Fincham *et al.*, 2010: 5) since it allows researchers the opportunity to observe participants but also sanctions a physical co-presence concerning the proximity of events. Drawing on this type of method means that the research being carried out is inevitably epistemologically linked with mobility since its relevance cannot be repudiated (Novoa, 2015). Doing mobile ethnography comprises a vast spectrum of activities ranging from shadowing participants' daily lives or workdays (Czarniawska, 2007) to engaging with their involvement of 'cross-border mobility' (Novoa, 2015: 100). The researcher is involved in a process of 'co-present immersion' moving around with informants and engaging in methods that include 'participation-while-interviewing' as well as a range of observation and recording techniques (Urry, 2007: 40). For Novoa (2015: 99), mobile ethnography is a:

> translation of traditional participant observation onto contexts of mobility. It means that the ethnographer is not only expected to observe what is happening, but also to experience, feel and grasp the textures, smells, comforts and discomforts, pleasures and displeasures of a moving life

In addition to moving around with Magda and shadowing her informally for years and very intensely when we carried out our official fieldwork in 2011 and 2015, we also visited customers and interviewed Magda's employees at Shine's headquarters, which is also Magda's home. Of course, we wanted to gain insight into the lives of the people we spoke to, and this meant making a conscious effort to capture the complexities within their workplace, but also their lives outside of work, which led us to their local neighborhoods of Elizabeth and Newark's Ironbound district (see Chapter 1 for a discussion).

2.7 Critical and Post-Critical Ethnography: Interpretive Stances, Reflexivity and Positionality

Drawing on critical ethnography means taking an interpretivist stance based on the ontological underpinnings of poststructuralist realism concerned with the ways in which individuals use language to construct their social worlds. Engaging in post-critical ethnography calls for being reflexive about the type of work we are carrying out and acknowledging that as researchers, our own positionalities, identities and interests influence our research agenda (Gonçalves & Schluter, 2017; Noblit *et al.*, 2004; Schluter, 2020). Using critical ethnographic methods compels us to think about our work and how it contributes to the equality and justice of our participants and our commitment to social change (Martin-Jones & Martin, 2017) although we are as of yet unaware of the kind of social change that can actually be done within the context of a small private business (see Section 2.5). This approach also heightens the relevance of our own positionality. As researchers, we are aware that our status as 'insiders' and 'outsiders' have advantages and disadvantages for our investigation (Carling *et al.*, 2014; Lanza, 2008; Zentella, 1997). This awareness calls for conducting ethically sound and responsible research among domestic workers and transnational labor migrants while simultaneously acknowledging the ways in which our relationships and collaboration with all participants affect the fieldwork process in particular and shape the overall research design.

According to Madison (2012: 6), 'critical ethnography begins with the ethical responsibility to address processes of unfairness or injustice within a particular *lived* domain'. As a critical ethnographer, one is committed to bringing to light the social injustices of human beings, giving voice to those who may not necessarily be heard and ultimately contributing to the social changes required for individuals regarding 'greater freedom and equity' (2012: 6).

As such, the critical ethnographer 'resists domestication and moves from "what is" to "what could be"' (2012: 5; Denzin, 2001; Thomas, 1993). In this endeavor, the researcher's positionality must always be accounted for.

Within qualitative research, Fine (1994) outlines three positions the researcher can take up:

1. The ventriloquist stance, which transmits information in an effort toward neutrality and is absent of a political or rhetorical stance. The position of the ethnographer aims to be invisible, that is, the 'self' strives to be non-existent in the text.
2. The positionality of the voiced stance is where subjects themselves are the focus, and their voices carry forward indigenous meanings and experiences that are in opposition to dominant discourses and practices. The position of the ethnographer is vaguely present but not addressed.
3. The activism stance in which the ethnographer takes a clear position in intervening on hegemonic practices and serves as an advocate in exposing the material effects of marginalized locations while offering alternatives.

(Fine, 1994: 17, as cited in Madison, 2012: 7)

These three points are similar to Habermas's (1971) positions of social inquiry that parallel (a) the natural science model, (b) the historical and interpretive model and (c) the critical theory model. For Madison (2012: 7), 'the critical theory model regards social life as being represented and analyzed for the political purpose of overcoming social oppression, particularly forms that reflect advanced capitalism through the overt polemics of the researcher'. According to Noblit *et al.* (2004: 4) 'we should not choose between critical theory and ethnography. Instead, we see that researchers are cutting new paths to re-inscribing critique in ethnography'. The stance we take in this project is a mixed one between points 2 and 3.

Different types of ethnography and stances enabled us to move forward with this project. Rather than claiming to do one type of ethnography, we opted for an approach that allowed us to mesh principles of mobile and critical ethnography with those of post-critical ethnography, which foreground our positionalities as researchers and the shifting nature of our positionalities over time.

2.8 Temporality within Ethnography: The Longitudinal Aspects of Our Study

One of the main concerns we have as ethnographers is the notion of time, in order to observe firsthand and try to understand better what Malinowski referred to as 'the imponderabelia of actual life' (Malinowski, 1922: 18). For us, the beauty of ethnography is undeniably its longitudinal dimension rather than engaging in so-called 'parachute anthropology' (Pedelty, 2004). From our perspective, engaging in ethnographic fieldwork gives researchers the time necessary to observe certain sociocultural and linguistic phenomena, experience predictable changes as well as deal with unexpected occurrences. Most importantly, though, ethnography allows us the ability to potentially tell a more 'complete' and richer story of the specific sociocultural phenomenon under investigation precisely due to its temporal aspect. In her description of ethnographies of bilingualism, Heller (2008: 250) states that 'fundamentally, ethnographies allow us to get at things we would otherwise never be able to discover'. This is certainly the case with care work and domestic labor contexts more specifically (Chang, 2000; Gonçalves & Schluter, 2020; Kaiper-Marquez & Makoni, 2022; Lan, 2006; Lorente, 2017; Lutz, 2011; Rollins, 1985). To claim that doing ethnography is holistic, however, has been met with contestation. For Heller (2008: 251) 'there is no such thing as a bounded whole, there are only processes which link together across space and time (Giddens, 1984)'. As such, we must keep in mind that ethnographies are parts – or perhaps even slices – of stories that change over time. They may be captured by the researcher since he or she cannot be extracted from it (DeFina, 2003).

For the ethnographer, time is an essential factor for one's study, from the beginning of one's research design continuing right down to the study's 'completion'. We specifically put completion in quotation marks because although ethnographers' projects might finish due to funding, institutional constraints, participants' or researchers' moving away and an array of other possible reasons, our curiosity often persists, and many studies continue off the record because we simply just cannot let them go. Essentially, we want to know how the story continues because the stories we tell in our ethnographic studies are about people and the relevant social, cultural, political, economic and linguistic issues and challenges they are confronted with. Moreover, we have developed relationships with the participants that transcend the confines of the project's duration. Their lived experiences are voiced through language. They are often discursively marked and framed in different but salient ways. The sociolinguistic issues taken up by us as researchers in many ways reflect their voices, which deserve to be heard. Often their voices might only be heard by other academics through their inclusion in the talks we give, the articles we publish or the books we write. This book is a compilation of snippets of stories that we consider timely and even a bit overdue. As with most ethnographic studies, we are well aware that the stories told in this book are indeed our own interpretations of them, which are being recounted here.

2.9 Chapter Summary

We began this chapter by revealing Kellie's close familial relationship with Magda, which was significant with regard to gaining access to Shine for our research purposes. While gaining access to individuals and a research site is crucial to any ethnographic project, in this chapter we also discussed the methodological disadvantages of this project as a result of Kellie's close relationship to Magda and many of Shine's employees (included in Table 2.1). We discussed how we are fully aware that our status and positionalities as 'insiders' and 'outsiders' compromised the objectivity of our analysis throughout this project. Afterward, we outlined the key methodological approaches used in this study, which consisted of mobile, critical and post-critical ethnography in order to gain a deeper insight into the workings of Shine from different perspectives. For this project, we also collected a number of different data sets that align with ethnographic research, which include participant observation and field notes, surveys conducted with Shine's clients, Shine's company booklet and interviews with all of Shine's employees, Magda, as well as several of Shine's clients. This mixed data set allowed for triangulation and the ability to cross-reference, which was especially relevant in this study since we were not afforded the opportunity to record interactions between domestic workers and clients. In terms of our analytical framework, we drew on both content and discourse analysis in order to identify common themes and linguistic patterns and the ways in which language functions among interlocutors in the co-construction and negotiation of social meaning. While one of our aims in this book is to give 'voice' to underrepresented individuals, we are fully aware that this is not 100% possible and that our analyses are based on snippets of stories from the various participants within this study, which are our own interpretations of them, recounted in the remainder of this book.

3 Magda: The Personal and Professional Trajectory of Shine's Owner

3.1 Introduction

One of the nice things about writing a book is that you can elaborate on certain themes and topics that until now have only been mentioned in passing. This is especially the case with Magda, Shine's owner. In our previous work (Gonçalves & Schluter, 2017), our discussion about Magda largely centers around the ways in which she manages her company logistically and linguistically. We investigate the ways in which she micromanages communication via brokering between different groups of people – for example, between her Anglophone clients and Portuguese and Spanish-speaking migrant employees – for company-external communication purposes. We also explored how communication was managed within and among her migrant employees who speak different languages (Portuguese and Spanish) as well as different language varieties (European Portuguese and Brazilian Portuguese speakers) through what we term 'inter-employee brokering' (Gonçalves & Schluter, 2017).

Through our investigation, we showed how Magda draws on direct language (Li, 1986), direct reported speech (Coulmas, 1986) and the use of directives (Vine, 2009), which demonstrates her agentive voice (Ahearn, 2001; Ortner, 1989; Ricento, 2000) and sheds light on the existing asymmetrical relations of power between Shine's employees, customers and even Magda herself. The image of Magda that has been constructed through our analyses so far has been one of a dominant female figure and no-nonsense businesswoman, who at times, takes on quite an authoritative leadership style vis-à-vis her employees and in some cases, also her customers. We know, however, through our own personal relationships with her and through our own observations (between Magda and her employees and Magda and her customers) that Magda also has a very soft, empathetic and personable side to her, which has been vital to her business's success.

In this chapter, in addition to showing her no-nonsense business leadership style, we also explore Magda's 'softer side' through our discussion of emotional intelligence. This exploration addresses the extent to which the various components of emotional intelligence according to Goleman (2000, 2015), which consist of *self-awareness*, *self-regulation*, *motivation*, *empathy* and *social skills*, pertain to Magda. We argue that Magda's high level of emotional intelligence, which she has acquired throughout her life, contributes to her dynamic leadership style within Shine. In this chapter, our aim is to illuminate Magda's multifaceted identities as a female, migrant business owner by tracing both her personal and professional trajectories as a transnational migrant and successful entrepreneur. These insights provide a deeper and more nuanced picture of Magda overall.

Providing readers (and ourselves as authors) with a well-balanced depiction of Magda has meant discussing Magda's past with her in numerous conversations over the years, to yield what some might refer to as life stories (Divita, 2021; Linde, 1993; McAdams, 2001) or a kind of biographical narrative. From an ethnographic perspective, tracing Magda's past life experiences has assisted us with understanding why and how she established Shine in the first place and provided us with key insights into how she has successfully managed her multilingual company for over 30 years. Indeed, as we already mentioned in Chapter 2, the insights provided by Magda presented in this chapter are recounted here for readers, and these are our own reiterations of them. Listening to Magda narrate about her past has assisted us with gaining a broader and more complex picture of Magda as a successful female migrant entrepreneur, who, like many of her employees, initially left Brazil (her home country) to work abroad as a domestic worker. In Magda's case, she was a live-in nanny in the 1970s. In the following sections, we provide ethnographic and biographical data of Magda for readers to gain better insight into her own transnational journey, which we believe has highly influenced Magda's emotional intelligence as a child, young adult and, subsequently, as a migrant, female business owner in the US.

3.2 Tracing Magda's History: From Childhood up to Her Formative Years

Magda was born in 1945 in the Brazilian highlands of Minas Gerais. She is the oldest of 10 children and until the age of seven was raised on her family's farm that economically survived by selling sugar cane, coffee and cattle to the domestic market. Although her immediate family was considered modest in terms of socioeconomic class, Magda and her family grew up with domestic workers, who helped cook, clean and tend to the children. The low cost of domestic labor within Brazil means that domestic workers are accessible to families from a wide range of socioeconomic backgrounds (see Gonçalves, 2022). In talking about her childhood and upbringing with us, Magda also mentioned that her grandfather was one of the wealthiest farmers and landowners in the region. Three of his daughters had attended Colegio Sacramentino de Manhumirim in Minas

Gerais, an upper-class Catholic boarding school located approximately 300 kilometers from their families' farms. Since Magda was the oldest granddaughter, her grandfather generously financed her tuition fee to attend this same boarding school. In 1952, when Magda was just seven years old, she left home to receive a better education than the local educational system could offer at the time. Due to the boarding school's regulations and Magda's familial financial means, she was permitted to go home to her family just twice a year, i.e. during Christmas and summer breaks. Magda talks about her time away and separation from her family at such an early age as both psychologically and emotionally challenging. The physical distance and long absences, coupled with the Catholic ideologies being taught at her school, created and maintained what she refers to as 'a rift' with most of her family members, whom she claims, she 'never really knew well'. While she was away at boarding school, most of her siblings were left behind to help work and tend to the farm.

In talking about her time at this boarding school, Magda discusses the sharp socioeconomic divisions that existed between the students. Those with the financial means were able to leave on weekends and visit their families while the financially less fortunate students were enrolled in what she refers to as a type of 'orphanage'. According to Magda, treatment among the student body was not equal and in one of our talks, she states:

Extract (1)

1. We were the slaves for the rich! We cleaned their quarters, their dorms, their study rooms and their
2. recreation quarters. The only thing is that we attended the same classrooms that they did. In the
3. classrooms, we were placed in the back of the class, and we also wore different uniforms, so that
4. everybody knew, who was rich and who was poor. I had excellent grades...except for behavior.

From this extract, we get a glimpse into Magda's childhood and her early experiences of carrying out domestic work for wealthier peers as well as the unequal treatment she and her similarly disadvantaged classmates experienced at this boarding school. Despite receiving an equal education to that of wealthy classmates, inequality was visually manifested in the classrooms. According to Magda, she and other 'poor' girls were semiotically marked through their different attire and physical/spatial separation in classrooms. While Magda excelled academically, she was often chastised and reprimanded for not abiding by the school's strict rules and disciplinary regulations resulting in low marks for social behavior.

In our talk, Magda attests to acting out and misbehaving as a result of what she considered at the time to be very unfair treatment and unjust expectations from school authorities, many of whom were Catholic nuns and, according to her, lacked empathy. Magda's outspokenness and inability to regulate her emotions often got her into trouble at school and eventually at home, but she was adamant about voicing her concerns regardless of the consequences, including the physical punishment she often endured as a result. Magda's experience at this boarding school shaped her moral and personal values about individuals, social injustices and especially empathy within a religious setting. She focused on her academics and looked forward to graduating and returning home.

3.3 Life-Changing Experiences and Young Adulthood: Family Tragedy, A Scholarship and Moving to the City

In this section, we discuss life-altering experiences, which Magda experienced at a young age, which altered her life's course. In 1960 when Magda was 15 years old, tragedy struck, and Magda's mother (who was pregnant with her eleventh child at the time) died due to birth complications, thus drastically affecting Magda's family life. Although Magda remained at home to attend her mother's funeral and help look after her siblings, she was soon ordered by her father to return to school and complete her education in the hope that she would one day be able to help support her family. Upon graduating from the Catholic boarding school with high marks, Magda enrolled in a university preparatory course in a city located about an hour away from her family's farm. A year later, she was permanently hired by her cousin, a high school administrator, to teach both history and math at the local high school in Divinolândia de Minas, a small town about eight kilometers from Magda's family farm. In 1967, she received a government-funded grant to study math at the Federal University of Minas Gerais (UFMG) in Belo Horizonte, the capital of Minas Gerais state for six months. This program was primarily aimed at continuing education for high school teachers. With all expenses covered, Magda took unpaid leave from her teaching position at the high school, moved to the city and enrolled in the course with the intention of returning and continuing her teaching career. With just two weeks left before the course's completion Magda saw an advertisement for another potential job opportunity, she states:

Extract (2)
1. It was a Sunday morning and I was sitting in front of the TV when I saw an announcement regarding
2. an *inscriçao* (application) for a job at the Department of Transportation in Belo Horizonte (BH). The
3. announcement was, 'Tomorrow is the last day for whoever is interested in doing the tests for the

4. vacancies at the Department of Transportation for BH'. I thought to myself, 'I have never done such a
5. kind of test, so I am going to go to the specified location and make my *inscriçao*
6. (application) tomorrow' and I did.

According to Magda, these federal job vacancies were extremely competitive. For just five vacancies, 3500 candidates had applied. Magda placed second overall and had achieved the highest possible scores in all categories except for typing. Magda was extremely motivated to continue her professional experience and received an immediate job offer to work in a law firm together with three state prosecutors. With her new, exciting and challenging job offer together with her university math certificate, she had to give her cousin the news that she would no longer be returning to Divinolândia, but staying in Belo Horizonte. She states, 'I explained to him that my opportunities in the capital were bigger than in a small town. I even offered to pay back little by little but he understood'. By remaining in the city rather than returning to her former job as a high school teacher, she knew she was putting her cousin in a difficult position. While he had covered her courses during her planned six-month hiatus, he now had to look into hiring a new permanent staff member. Magda knew that such a position was difficult to fill but had the social skills (a main component of emotional intelligence) necessary to relay the news to him in a professional manner by being honest about her goals and suggesting she reimburse him for his troubles, an offer she felt was fair in exchange for his generous proposal to keep her job when she returned.

Magda worked for these three lawyers in Belo Horizonte from 1968 until the mid-1970s and enjoyed the challenges of her new job as a legal secretary and assistant. As Magda's knowledge and curiosity about Brazilian law increased, so did her motivation to study it. Her professional diligence was evident in her new workplace, so much so that one lawyer agreed to pay her full tuition to attend law school. This promise and potential opportunity also coincided with another job offer to move to the US and work as a live-in nanny for an upper-class Brazilian family, who owned a private pediatrics practice in Newark, New Jersey.

3.4 Transnational Migration and Private Language Planning: Magda's Own Domestic Worker Experience in the US

The upper-class Brazilian family who offered Magda a job in the US did so for reasons of private language planning (see Curdt-Christiansen, 2018; Gonçalves & Lanza, forthcoming; Wright & Higgens, 2022, for recent studies on family language policy) to ensure the transmission of Portuguese to their two young daughters. The family offered Magda a job to work for them as a part-time nanny for the children and a secretary/assistant at the doctor's private practice. In both cases her Portuguese language proficiency was an important aspect and asset of the position. Magda was originally reluctant to accept this offer as she had had hopes of attending law school, eventually marrying her fiancé and thus remaining in Brazil. She states:

Extract (3)

1. I knew some British English and dreamed about going to England one day, but never had a desire
2. and it had never crossed my mind to go to the US, but after talks and talks from both doctors
3. I decided 'ok, I'll go' but, but salary was never one of the discussions.

Choosing to uproot to move to the US and delay her studies in law was a decision that Magda made based on the experience and skills she would accrue in the US. One of these skills included learning English. She told herself that two years would pass by quickly, and her fiancé would also patiently wait for her return as would the kind offer from her employer to finance her law degree. As Magda recounts, being separated from family and loved ones was a familiar feeling from her childhood, and, therefore, the decision to finally set off to the US was not a difficult one to make. According to Magda, her new Brazilian employer organized everything associated with Magda's trip overseas, including her passport, visa and flight. Within weeks of accepting her new job, she was ready to travel overseas to meet the new family she would be working for and simultaneously living with. At the time of her arrival, the two children she was responsible for were four years old and six months old. Magda was shown around the private practice just once, and her actual work duties were confined primarily to the family's home, where she was expected to look after the children and complete other domestic duties like cooking, cleaning and doing the laundry. Although Magda had been informed that her job would incorporate tasks relating to both the family's children and private practice, she never worked in the latter capacity. With regards to the former, Magda stated, 'I watched the children and did all the housework. This went on for six months and I earned just $110.00 a month'. Additionally, Magda attended English classes at night and was able to do this since they were being offered locally free of charge. Learning English for Magda became the key to her upward social mobility, which we discuss in the following section.

3.5 From Nanny to Entrepreneur: The Hegemonic Discourse of Learning English: The Key to Magda's Upward Social Mobility and Professional Identities

For Magda, attending English classes at night proved to be both a neoliberal educational pursuit and social endeavor (Block *et al.*, 2012;

De Costa *et al.*, 2016, 2018, 2021; Lorente, 2017; Martín Rojo & Del Percio, 2020; Norton, 2000; Pujolar, 2020). Magda's English classes were a time and place where English communication skills were regarded as reified, much like languages, in terms of being countable and separate entities (García *et al.*, 2017; Gonçalves, 2020a; Makoni & Pennycook, 2007; Spotti *et al.*, 2019), which had instrumental value that could be learned or acquired through formal instruction. Magda's classes also simultaneously served as a social hub where friendships were made and romantic bonds were formed. Through her friendship with Rosa, a Brazilian classmate, she gained some insight into her working conditions. Rosa and Magda's close affinity allowed Magda to open up to her about her current situation, where she felt manipulated as a domestic worker, Magda states:

Extract (4)

1. One day I told her my story and she said, 'Oh my God, these people are taking such advantage of you,
2. I am going to talk to my mother and I will call you tomorrow'. I managed to take a day off on a Wednesday and
3. Rosa's mom took me to the Social Security Office and I walked out of that office with my social security number, it's
4. the same number as I have today. She could not believe what that family was doing to me and she said that she knew
5. someone that was working for a family and she was earning, not much but $350.00 a month. She also knew someone
6. who worked and had a high position at C & D Paint Company and she got me a job there for me, in the laboratory.
7. I worked for two chemical engineers and also with Nick and Dania, my Polish friends to this day. Our job was to help
8. the engineers to discover formulas for new paint colors.

During this transitional time in Magda's life, she rented a room and lived with a fellow Brazilian in Newark, New Jersey. Her working duties were ones in which she used primarily English and a time during which, according to her, her 'English improved tremendously' as the two engineers and co-workers on her team unit were American. Magda continued to take English classes in the evening and also eventually met a European Portuguese man, Alberto, with whom she became romantically involved. With her social security card in hand, Magda decided in 1973 that it was time to go back to Brazil, tie up all loose ends and introduce her family to her new Portuguese fiancé. Magda and Alberto were married in Brazil and later returned to Elizabeth, New Jersey, to live with her in-laws. Upon their return from Brazil, Magda was an employee at a clothing factory, having got the job through her mother-in-law, who also worked there. The time spent at the clothing factory was short-lived since Magda was pregnant with her first child who was born in April of 1974. By August of the same year, Magda received an offer from Santos Bank in Elizabeth, New Jersey, to work as a receptionist. Magda states, 'I knew nothing about banking but erm at that time the bank was in need of someone who spoke Portuguese as their customers were 80% Portuguese and Spanish [speakers] so I was hired'. In recounting her early days at the bank, Magda alludes to her insecurities about speaking English in an institutional setting where her job and ensuing language abilities were no longer 'backstage performances' (Goffman, 1957) as they had been in her previous positions in the laboratory or factory. Instead, she was now a part of the face of the company.

Being a receptionist at an American bank meant that she had to draw on the entirety of her linguistic repertoire to accomplish tasks, depending on what clients required. While she was initially hired to do specific language brokering and translating work for Portuguese- and Spanish-speaking clients, her position and role at the bank soon changed. This promotion may have resulted from Magda's emotional intelligence, confidence and ability to navigate customers' concerns, which she could handle and resolve, regardless of customers' first language (L1). Magda indicated that practicing her English-language skills with customers on the phone improved her communication abilities over time. By overcoming her initial anxiety about talking on the phone with potential customers, Magda eventually used these opportunities to practice and 'perfect' her English banking skills with them. With regards to how this was done, Magda states the following:

Extract (5)

1. The customers at the bank erm were like 80% either Portuguese or Spanish and erm this girl was erm
2. pregnant and she was leaving and erm they needed somebody to you know speak with Portuguese
3. customers that spoke no English at all when they came to open accounts so I knew how to speak, but
4. you know? Not almost maybe less than I know today but erm (laughter), but so, I, I you know I was given
5. the job of receptionist so of course everybody that came to me most people were like Portuguese,
6. Spanish but when the phone ringed I looked around, we were like a big office like about 12 people total
7. erm in the office and erm when the phone ringed, I didn't know if they were going to speak which
8. language and one day the phone was ringing and ringing and ringing and I looked and everybody was

9. on the phone so I had to pick up that phone and that broke the ice, from that day on, you know? As
10. soon as that phone ringed, I said, 'Oh, let me grab it' and I, I had no fear of speaking anymore.

Being forced to deploy her English-language abilities on the phone was regarded by Magda as an icebreaker, where panic and anxiety surrounding grammar and pronunciation were quickly overcome. Magda's renewed sense of confidence and linguistic abilities, coupled with a higher salary than her previous jobs, allowed her to be financially independent and motivated to work hard. Unhappy living with her in-laws, she decided to move. With the assistance of a colleague and friend, she leased an apartment for her husband, their daughter and herself. In discussing this moment of time in her life, Magda states, 'I told my husband that I had leased an apartment and was moving with Jane. If he wanted to go, it was fine, but if he didn't, it was fine too. We moved'. Here, we are introduced to Magda as an *entrepreneurial subject*, who takes charge and is responsible for governing her own resources and assets (Martín Rojo, 2020). At this point, we also become familiar with the emotionally intelligent, independent, agentive and no-nonsense side of Magda as it pertains to her personal life, which we have also witnessed numerous times at Shine with regard to her leadership and management style. From this extract, we may better understand how her past experiences, life challenges and the hegemonic discourses at the time (English-language competence for upward social mobility), combined with different stories of success, initiated the change needed for self-improvement in order for Magda to feel fulfilled, comfortable and independent in her new American life. As a Brazilian female migrant, mother, wife and bank employee, who was experiencing social mobility within her workplace as a result of her acquired emotional intelligence, multilingual abilities, educational qualifications and previous employment experience, she could be considered the hallmark of what Martín Rojo (2020) refers to as the 'self-made speaker' and in line with the work of De Costa *et al.* (2016, 2018) on linguistic entrepreneurship. In fact, the financially independent woman she and her father had once hoped for had in many ways materialized. Magda had accumulated the necessary cultural capital to navigate the banking domain within a US context, which helped lay the foundation for her future role as a female, migrant entrepreneur. Throughout her nearly decade-long career in banking, Magda experienced upward social mobility as she rose from receptionist, assistant secretary, assistant manager, branch manager and, finally, to operations manager. During her time as operations manager at the branch in Short Hills (an affluent suburb of New York City), she was offered a promotion to operations manager in a much larger bank in Elizabeth, New Jersey. In this capacity, she would oversee 26 employees, but she turned it down. In our interview, she states the following:

Extract (6)

1. Magda: they actually wanted to transfer me as a manager there and erm…but the environment and I
2. knew, you know, just like having two kids erm, it would be too much work because I knew, I had
3. worked there like for eight years before and I knew, you know, erm how much work and I said, 'no, I
4. don't want the position', so I guess to punish me, they said that erm my position at Short Hills, I was at
5. the level that I could not have no raises anymore, the regional manager, erm and, and it's all politics I
6. mean, I said, no to her and she said, 'Wow, you know? Nobody says no', so I realized that erm no matter
7. what I did there, you know, they're just gonna you know?
8. Kellie: keep you at that level?
9. Magda: keep me at that level monetarily you know? I would do a lot of work, but they would not raise
10. my salary…so…with a divorce, I had to find a way to make more money and erm it came at a time that
11. I had like an accumulation of vacation for a month so I said, 'Well, I'm going to take this vacation and
12. start this business' and what really gave me the idea about the business was like my own customers
13. at the bank that would come and say, 'Hey, Magda, do you know somebody who cleans?' […] so, I said,
14. 'well, it seems like there's erm a demand you know for this business' and erm since I had the vacation
15. for a month, I said, 'I'm gonna start it, if it works, fine, if it doesn't work, you know, I'll go back to erm
16. the bank', so I never went back…it worked, yeah

In this extract, we are introduced to the various factors that contributed to Shine's establishment. As a single mother of two children, Magda's financial situation changed drastically. However, accepting the offered promotion at the Elizabeth bank branch was undesirable due to the increased working hours and commute time, which would mean more time away from her young children (lines 2–4). By remaining in her current position at Short Hills, she professionally and financially plateaued. Because Magda had previously worked in the Elizabeth branch, she was still familiar with many of the co-workers and also the challenges of managing that specific branch. After some deliberation and repeated requests from customers for contact with her network of domestic workers (line 13), Magda saw a business opportunity she felt was worth pursuing (lines 14–16).

In discussing Shine's establishment with us, Magda stated that the response to her business was 'overwhelming'. Although it was the first time she was managing her own business, Magda was equipped with the necessary financial, management, emotional, social, cultural and linguistic competences through her numerous positions at the bank to run a small and quickly growing cleaning service. She became both an empathetic yet authoritative entrepreneur and leader, which we discuss in the following section.

3.6 Leadership, Empathy and Emotional Intelligence: 'The Softer Side' of Magda

Literature on both entrepreneurship and leadership has been investigated for decades from a predominately Western perspective. The foci have largely been on business creation and success and analyzed primarily from a normative (male) standpoint (Ogbor, 2000; Williams & Nadin, 2013). More recent work (Galloway *et al.*, 2015) has called for a greater and wider exploration of leadership, entrepreneurship and 'entrepreneurial leadership' from a feminist perspective. This view underscores the salience of performativity among leaders and thus rejects gender essentialization, while at the same time, calling for emotional intelligence, a feature that is culturally marked as female (Galloway *et al.*, 2015; Mandell & Pherwani, 2003). Although there is a lot of work and a growing interest in language and workplace studies within the field of sociolinguistics, relatively few studies have focused on communication among colleagues, peers and employers (although see papers in Canagarajah [2020] and the work of Söderlundh and Keevalik [2022]). The work of Holmes *et al.* (2011) on leadership, discourse and ethnicity within New Zealand workplaces is an exception. At the same time, these scholars also maintain that despite the pre-existing literature, 'there has been relatively little research that focuses on how people actually communicate verbally with their colleagues at work on a daily basis, and even less on how leaders use talk to accomplish their objectives' (2011: 22). While their discursive analyses focus on the micro-level with regard to various competencies, stances and identity formations connected to effective leadership, our focus in this chapter with Magda encompasses a broader discussion of emotional intelligence as it pertains to contemporary leadership studies as well as sociolinguistic studies concerned with language and the workplace.

In his best-selling book titled *Leaders Eat Last: Why Some Teams Pull Together and Others Don't*, Sinek (2014) draws on several stories of the military to discuss characteristics of good leadership and successful organizations and workplaces. He describes in detail the ways in which some organizations fail while others thrive in different socioeconomic, cultural and political contexts and unpredictable circumstances. He maintains that it is a result of the company's organizational culture that is created and maintained from the top-down and influences every level of an organization. He states (2014: 8):

> There is a pattern that exists in the organizations that achieve the greatest success, the ones that outmaneuver and outinnovate their competitors, the ones that command the greatest respect from inside and outside their organizations, the ones with the highest loyalty and lowest churn and the ability to weather nearly every storm or challenge. These exceptional organizations all have cultures in which leaders provide cover from above and the people on the ground look out for each other. This is the reason they are willing to push hard and take the kind of risks they do. And the way any organization can achieve this is with empathy.

When reading through this extract, we are reminded of how Magda navigates her business and also manages her customers and employees (Gonçalves & Schluter, 2017). Although Magda at times has a very authoritative style of leadership which will emerge later on in this chapter, it is balanced by her emotional intelligence and empathy toward both her customers and employees. What Sinek states about leaders 'providing cover from above' was what we also witnessed at Shine numerous times. One example is when Magda canceled a house because her client accused the cleaning lady of losing a puzzle piece. While we discuss this example and how Magda dealt with it in more detail in Section 3.9.1 (Magda-customer power relations), it is a prime example of her 'providing cover from above' for her employees against insulting comments and behavior from clients. Most of Magda's employees are diligent, trustworthy and dedicated to their work, enabling Shine to be a successful organization and workplace. This comes from Magda's ability to lead her company in a way that often resembles a family, which is tight-knit, loyal and caring despite her overt favoritism toward Portuguese employees. Over the years we have witnessed the thoughtful, attentive and soft side of Magda as it pertains to both her customers and employees. The next extract, taken from Kellie's field notes, highlights this point in particular:

Extract (7)

> Today I went with Magda to Bart's, the local drugstore in Westwood, because she needed to buy some cards. Initially I thought this would be a quick errand, but it turned out to be quite a long trip. While I looked around at various toiletries and rows of candy I wanted to buy and take back home with me, Magda stood in the card section for nearly an hour carefully reading and selecting cards for various individuals, her basket filled with vibrant and dull-colored envelopes. When I asked her who the cards were

for, she proceeded to give me a long list of recipients composed of customers who were sick or whose parent had recently passed away to employee's children who were celebrating upcoming confirmations and sweet-sixteens. She never misses an occasion to reach out to people. This was not the first time I had witnessed Magda's social skills and empathy, but it has always surprised me that she is able to cater to both her clients and employees' very diverse and often complex lives outside of the workplace domain and maintain the personal aspects in all of these relationships (June 2016).

Whether it is giving an ill elderly client (cf. extract with Mrs Gloski) an exception with regards to their weekly cleaning schedule or assisting an employee with a move following a divorce, Magda has prioritized personal relationships both inside and outside of Shine and nurtured these relationships through her own self-awareness and empathy toward others, two main components of emotional intelligence.

3.7 Emotional Intelligence: A Model to Understand Magda's Leadership Style at Shine

In this section, we describe in detail the various components of emotional intelligence as they have been understood and outlined by Goleman (2000, 2015). We do this first by discussing his model as it pertains to successful and effective leadership in general and then, more specifically, as it concerns Magda and her leadership style within Shine. According to Goleman (2015: 1), 'emotional intelligence is the *sine qua non* of leadership' and 'without it, a person can have the best training in the world, an incisive, analytic mind, and an endless supply of smart ideas' but will inevitably fail at being able to lead effectively. Researchers have found that emotional intelligence could be more relevant than individuals' IQs and expertise (see Sadri, 2012, for an overview), and according to Goleman (2015: 27), the significance of emotional intelligence can be found 'across all categories of jobs, and in all kinds of organizations'. Indeed, the debate about whether emotional intelligence can be learned or if one is born with it continues to be disputed (Burcea & Sabie, 2020; Conger, 2004; Sadri, 2012). Researchers such as Murphy (2006) believe there is still a long way to go in terms of testing individuals for their levels of emotional intelligence. However, research has shown the effectiveness of emotional intelligence by leaders and that it can indeed be learned through specific sociocultural training and repetitive practice (Galloway *et al.*, 2015; Goleman, 1998, 2000, 2015; Nixon *et al.*, 2012). According to Goleman (2015: 8), emotional intelligence is 'born largely in the neurotransmitters of the brains' limbic system, which governs feelings, impulses, and drives'. In his research Goleman and his colleagues have focused on how emotional intelligence operates at work and, more specifically, how the relationship between emotional intelligence and effective

Table 3.1 Emotional Intelligence according to Goleman's (1998, 2000, 2015) five features

Component	Definition
(1) Self-Awareness	The ability to recognize and understand your moods, emotions and drives, as well as their effect on others
(2) Self-Regulation	The ability to control or redirect disruptive impulses and moods; the ability to suspend judgment and think before acting
(3) Motivation	Exhibiting a passion to work for reasons outside money or status; a drive to pursue goals with energy and persistence
(4) Empathy	The ability to understand the emotional makeup of others; skills in treating others according to their emotional reactions
(5) Social skills	Capable of managing relationships and building networks; able to find common ground and build a relationship

performance functions within leaders. Although these studies have been conducted primarily within large corporate contexts and emotional intelligence is still an evolving area of theory, we contend that it is relevant for the discussion of Magda as an effective leader within Shine, a small private business. In Table 3.1, we list Goleman's (1998, 2000, 2015) model of emotional intelligence and the foundational components required, which consist of *self-awareness*, *self-regulation*, *motivation*, *empathy* and *social skills*. We go through each of these components in turn and provide an example of how these features factor into Magda's effective leadership style based on our own observations and interview data.

3.7.1 Emotional intelligence component 1: Self-awareness

According to Goleman, self-awareness means having a deep understanding of one's emotions, strengths, weaknesses, needs and drives. People with strong self-awareness are neither overly critical nor unrealistically hopeful. Rather, they are honest with themselves and with others. Being self-aware means that an individual possesses the ability to recognize and understand their moods, emotions and drives, as well as their effect on other individuals. Although the boundaries between self-awareness and other components of Goleman's emotional intelligence model are not always clear-cut, the component of self-awareness for Magda is one we witnessed repeatedly. Not only did we observe this firsthand through our observations of Magda and our interviews with her, but we were also informed about Magda's self-awareness through both her employees and customers. As we have already mentioned, Magda is a no-nonsense business woman, and she knows both what she wants and what she will not tolerate from both her employees and customers in order to optimize Shine's services. In these ways, and in line with the definition of self-awareness, Magda is honest about her choices and also very aware of how they will affect employees and customers. With regard to her employees, Magda acknowledges and frankly states 'I'm very demanding', indicating that she is aware of her own commanding nature as an employer. With regard to customers, she is also self-aware when it comes to customer relations and, for example, the canceling of houses. She states, 'Once I cancel a house, it's done'. Magda also does not service houses on her street or within a few blocks of her own house. The reason for this according to Magda is that she does not want to 'mix business with pleasure'. For her, the personal relations she has with her neighbors are amicable, and she is not willing to put them at risk for the sake of economic profit. In these ways, Magda recognizes her direct nature, and she is open about her management choices and Shine's policies. Indeed, one could argue that the examples mentioned above may counter other components of emotional intelligence, including self-regulation, empathy and social skills, but we argue that, in fact, Magda's direct style, coupled with her empathy and social skills, are key to the ways in which she has successfully managed her business.

3.7.2 Emotional intelligence component 2: Self-regulation

Self-regulation is the ability to regulate one's emotions. According to Goleman (2015), people who are in control of their feelings and impulses are able to create an environment of trust and fairness. In such an environment, 'politics and infighting are sharply reduced and productivity is high' (2015: 12). Talented people flock to the organization and are not tempted to leave. For Goleman, self-regulation also has a trickle-down effect. For him, 'no one wants to be known as a hothead when the boss is known for their calm approach. Fewer bad moods at the top mean fewer throughout the organization' (2015: 12). Although we would not always characterize Magda as calm, we have witnessed both her ability and, in some instances, even her inability to regulate her emotions with regards to her responses to both employees and customers. Our time at Shine's headquarters as well as our time shadowing Magda has given us ample insight into Magda's emotional states during different times of the working day, seasons and years, allowing us to get a sense of her ability to self-regulate especially as it pertains to mundane everyday business scenarios and ensuing challenges. Examples include employees' inability to enter a house to clean due to pets (mainly dogs that were not secured), or alarm systems that customers had forgotten to deactivate, resulting in police squads surrounding the house. With regard to the former, we once experienced a scenario when a cleaning lady had been dropped off at a client's house that she had been cleaning for years on a regular, weekly basis. Usually, the dog was always kept in a pen in the basement but on this occasion, and upon entering the house, the domestic worker quickly realized that the dog had in fact been left loose and unattended. The domestic worker knew the rules about pets (which was that pets needed to be secured in crates or outside) and therefore called Magda immediately to inform her about the situation. Although we sensed Magda's initial annoyance, she was able to handle the situation in a self-controlled and diplomatic manner. In Shine's company booklet, customers are specifically informed to keep pets either caged or in the yard during Shine's services in order for the cleaning lady to work efficiently and undisturbed. Magda also explicitly states this to new customers upon taking on their houses. The unattended dog in this scenario clearly violated Shine's rules for customers, yet Magda was also understanding of her customers and knew that such mistakes can happen. When situations such as these arise, Magda reallocates the cleaning lady to another house and then informs the customer immediately either through a phone call or text message that their house could not be serviced. Magda states that if Shine's schedule allows the house to be cleaned on another day that same week, she tries to accommodate her customers' needs and requests rather than keep them waiting an entire week for their house to be serviced. In such instances, customers are also expected to pay the weekly cleaning fee and often do not have any objections since payment policies are explicitly stated in the company booklet. In fact, customers are often embarrassed and very apologetic toward Magda and her staff for the inconvenience caused and know that by not abiding by Shine's regulations, their house could potentially be terminated indefinitely. This example demonstrates Magda's ability to self-regulate impulses and moods. While she may be annoyed by such situations, she is able to handle them in a diplomatic manner in order to ensure that they do not happen on a regular basis.

For Goleman (2015), self-regulation also enhances integrity, which exceeds the personal virtues of leaders and extends into organizational strength. Magda's honesty toward her employees and customers has indeed permeated throughout Shine. We experienced this on several occasions when, for example, one of Shine's employees accidentally broke an item in a customer's house. The fact that Shine is insured and bonded means that Magda's staff is not liable for replacing broken items. When accidents occur in customers' houses, Magda's staff is also apologetic toward Magda and the customer. In these ways, self-regulation for a leader also has to do with the ability of individuals to be reflective, thoughtful and capable of ambiguity, change and integrity.

3.7.3 Emotional intelligence component 3: Motivation

The third component listed in Goleman's (2015) model is motivation, which is connected to a leader's drive. For Goleman, leaders who are motivated are also driven to achieve beyond their own and everyone else's expectations (2015: 14). When the leader's motivation and drive are high, these also extend to an organization's employees. Additionally, commitment is key, and it is also tied closely to achieving motivation. If leaders are committed to a cause and achievement – rather than through external factors such as money – within their organization, the feeling of commitment will also permeate throughout the organization.

When people enjoy and even love their jobs for the work itself, they often feel committed to the organizations that they work for. For Goleman, if employees are committed to their jobs, then they are also more likely to stay with the organization in the long run. When we were conducting our first round of interviews with Shine's employees in 2011, one relevant point emerged repeatedly: most of the cleaning ladies we spoke with talked about how much they liked their jobs. This was an answer that quite frankly we were not expecting to hear, but, over time, it became clear that Shine's employees enjoyed their jobs for numerous reasons. These reasons had to do with their working days and hours, the number of houses cleaned per day, the high-quality service Shine offered, the transportation service provided by Shine, and having Magda as a boss. Shine's low turnover rate is one indicator of individuals' satisfaction with their jobs. Over the years, Magda has been able to retain employees, some of whom have worked for Shine for over 10, 15 and 20 years. In fact, several cleaning ladies had been with Shine since its establishment.

3.7.4 Emotional intelligence component 4: Empathy

According to Goleman, empathy is a term we do not often hear within the context of business leaders; however, it is considered to be a crucial element of successful and effective leadership. For him, empathy is about 'thoughtfully considering employees' feelings – along with other factors – in the process of making intelligent decisions' (2015: 16). Within the business world, empathy is an important component of leadership for three main reasons: the increasing use of teams, the rapid pace of globalization and the growing need to retain talent. We contend that, indeed, all of these reasons are relevant for Magda and her employees within the context of Shine and, especially, as they pertain to the transnational and cross-cultural differences that influence communication practices. Due to Magda's previous work experience in multilingual, multicultural Elizabeth, New Jersey, as well as her decade-long marriage to a Portuguese man, Magda had learned the linguistic and paralinguistic differences between both Portuguese varieties (European and Luso-Brazilian) especially on the pragmatic level to be able to mediate between her employees and what we have called 'inter-employee' brokering (Gonçalves & Schluter, 2017). Magda has always been able to speak to Shine's employees both collectively and individually. On numerous occasions, Kellie has overheard face-to-face and telephone conversations between Magda and her employees. Talking things through openly allowed Magda direct access to the emotional makeup of her employees and the issues they were facing on a daily basis both inside and outside of the workplace. In fact, most of the challenges her employees face are not necessarily work-related, and Magda's apparent concern for their lives outside of work instills a feeling of loyalty to her. An example of this was when Adriana, Shine's assistant manager and driver, could not secure a childminder for her daughter, Julia, one month during the summer holidays.

Adriana is one of Shine's most important employees, who has been working for and with Magda for over 20 years (see Chapter 5 for a detailed discussion of Adriana). Adriana quickly rose within Shine's hierarchy due to her diligence, emotional intelligence and various social competences. While she is by no means fluent in English, her English proficiency skills, together with her optimism and upbeat attitude toward customers and co-workers, have contributed to her popularity and success within the company on both an individual and collective level. Without Adriana, Magda's management tasks would be much greater and, as a result, Magda stepped in to assist Adriana with her daughter that summer. Magda also knew that if Adriana missed a month of work, the resources needed to replace her would be significant. In order to retain Adriana at work (both uninterrupted and worry-free), Magda offered to be Julia's caretaker for the month. At the time, Julia was taking a summer course nearby that ended at noon. Magda offered to pick her up, take her to her own home, make her lunch, assist her with her homework and look after her until 4 pm, when Julia joined her mother and others as part of Shine's carpool to drive back home. Adriana accepted Magda's offer, and Adriana's day-care challenge and Magda's potential employee shortage were quickly resolved. As a single mother of two daughters, Magda was well aware of the parenting challenges during the summer holidays. In these ways, Magda was able to identify with Adriana's emotions and concerns and reacted empathetically toward Adriana and the difficult situation she found herself in. Interestingly enough, this joint time between Magda and Julia allowed them to develop an independent and nurturing relationship. As time passed, Julia gave Magda the nickname *vózinha*, the diminutive Portuguese term meaning 'little grandmother', to depict her. Subsequently, Julia has also joined Magda on family vacations and trips back to Brazil. The relationships that Magda has with both Adriana and Julia are strong and continue to this day. In fact, whenever Kellie visits Magda in New Jersey, she always meets up with Adriana's family at either their own home in Elizabeth or at Magda's home in Westwood. During our data collection session in 2015, we both went to Adriana's house for a home-cooked Portuguese meal. Indeed, these times of socialization granted us an inside perspective into the tightly knit relationships between Magda, Adriana and her family. Magda and Adriana have always had a compatible working relationship, which also extends into their personal relationship outside of work. This example demonstrates a way in which Magda's empathy is self-serving in that she too profits from this tight-knit relationship. Over the years, we also witnessed Magda's empathetic relationship with her employees that were also not self-serving such as when Magda organized a mattress and other furniture for an employee and her young child, who, after several years of marriage, was leaving her husband.

Over the years, Magda has continued to learn about contemporary European Portuguese usage through her relationship with her Portuguese employees and especially with Adriana and Julia. Magda told us the following anecdote, which comprises these cross-cultural semantic and pragmatic differences, which resulted in a humorous exchange:

Extract (8)

1. Magda: I was in the van and Adriana was with me. I was in a really tight parking spot and
2. couldn't see anything, you know, if cars were coming from either side so, so, she [Adriana]
3. got out of the car to help me. She was standing behind the car and shouted, '*vem do cu,*
4. *Dona Magda, vem do co*' (come from the ass, Dona Magda, come from the ass) (laughter).

Within European Portuguese varieties, the term *cu* is the equivalent of 'behind' but in Brazilian Portuguese, *cu* is considered to be an expletive/swearword, meaning 'ass'. While Magda was already familiar with the semantic and pragmatic differences of the word's meaning, she still found the phrase 'come from [the car's] ass' a humorous instance indexed by her laughter (line 4). For Goleman (2015: 18), 'cross-cultural dialogue can easily lead to miscues and misunderstandings and empathy is therefore an antidote'. For him, people who are equipped and attuned with cross-cultural differences and in individuals' body language are able to decipher implicit messages; 'beyond that, they have a deep understanding of both the existence and the importance of cultural and ethnic differences' (2015: 18). Through Magda's cross-cultural marriage and previous work experience, Magda is equipped with the necessary cross-cultural know-how and understanding of metalinguistic differences to navigate misunderstandings between her employees and between her employees and clients. An example of this can be found further in the chapter with regard to 'inter-employee brokering' (Gonçalves & Schluter, 2017), which may also be regarded as an instance in which empathy and intercultural competence are carried out and displayed between Magda and her employees.

According to Goleman (2015: 18–19),

> empathy doesn't get much respect in business. People wonder how leaders can make hard decisions if they are 'feeling' for all the people who will be affected. But leaders with empathy do more than sympathize with people around them: They use their knowledge to improve their companies in subtle but important ways.

Indeed, navigating between employees with different cultural and linguistic backgrounds, in essence being equipped with intercultural communicative competence, has been key for Magda's business which we have discussed at length in Gonçalves and Schluter (2017). Without her ability to engage in this kind of intercultural mediation, Shine would not be a prosperous small business. This fact, coupled with Magda's empathetic nature toward both her employees and customers, is another factor we believe contributes to Shine as an effective and highly sought-after service provider in both local and regional areas (which we discuss in further detail in Section 3.9.1).

3.7.5 Emotional intelligence component 5: Social skills

The final component of Goleman's model has to do with leaders' social skills. Social skills are associated with the ways in which a person is able to manage relationships with others. While social skills are indeed a component of empathy, it is not, according to Goleman, so simple (2015: 19). In fact, Goleman ascertains that social skills are not just about friendliness, but friendliness 'with a purpose'. Within the organization, the social skills required of a leader have to do with 'moving people in the direction you desire' (2015: 19). For Magda, this translates into her ability to navigate a wide range of relationships consisting of employee-employee, employee-customer, supervisor-employee and company head-customer. In fact, managing these relationships is absolutely vital to Magda's business and company culture.

In her recent book titled *Radical Candor: Be a Kick-Ass Boss Without Losing Your Humanity*, Scott (2017) describes a revolutionary framework for management within the corporate world and tech start-ups in particular. Having worked for Google, Apple and her own businesses, she contends that 'relationships are core to your job. If you think you can fulfill your responsibilities as a manager without strong relationships, you are kidding yourself' (2014: 113). Indeed, maintaining strong relationships for Magda is absolutely vital for Shine's success. This is also one of the main reasons why she decided to keep her business small and 'socially manageable' on a personal level rather than focus on continued growth and financial profit. At the peak of Shine's business, there were over 300 customers, 30 employees and five vans (and, thus, five drivers). At that time, Shine provided services regionally, with certain vans traveling beyond the Westwood area by another 15–30 miles. The logistics of this complex operation, according to Magda, were not only challenging to maintain with Magda as the sole owner and primary manager despite her assistant managers Bianca and Adriana. Magda soon realized the additional challenges of maintaining high-quality personal relationships with her staff and customers. This becomes clear in the following extract from one of our interviews, which aligns well with our field notes about Magda and her card buying for customers and employees:

Extract (9)

1. Kellie: I think one thing that's intrigued me...erm...about the business especially having
2. seen it through various stages erm...why not expand?
3. Magda: (laughter) oh (laughter) at my age?
4. Kellie: no, well, you could've, I mean, I'm saying, there was a time where you had more now
5. you've got 19? 18? [employees]
6. Magda: Oh yeah, there was a time we had like about 30-something people, yeah, but you know
7. we did Short Hills, we did Wayne, we did erm Watchung, Chatham and then you know? It's too
8. much because it's me, I mean the girls come, clean the house and they go home and you know,
9. the phone rings and there's this and there's that you know? It's, so, it's a lot of work, yeah
10. Kellie: but I think it's also, I mean something that...you've done over the years, you also like
11. to keep it very personal =[between you and your customers
12. Magda: =[exactly, I, I like to keep it small and personal, yeah...I am, if I stop
13. by a house for whatever reason I always have like a bunch of cards with me, blank cards that
14. I will leave a note for the customer and stuff like that
15. Kellie: [...] and you write, do you still write them personal Christmas cards?
16. Magda: oh yes, by hand...by hand, I did this from year number one and I think I want to do it
17. until, you know, til it's yeah...I write each individual Christmas card you know, dear Leslie,
18. dear Jill and you know, each one a note, not the same note to everybody
19. Anne: mhm
20. Kellie: yeah, you start in October?
21. Magda: yeah, it's almost time (laughter)

When it comes to her clients, Magda invests different resources in order to manage and maintain good personal customer relations. A case in point is her personal, hand-written notes to customers (lines 12–14) and annual personalized Christmas cards (lines 15–18). For Magda, her hand-written and personalized Christmas cards are a way to both acknowledge her customers and thank them for their continued loyalty. While it takes Magda nearly two-months' time to write these cards, namely, October to December (lines 20–21), Magda's investment and commitment to maintaining personal and, thus, social relationships among her customers is a point she has and continues to prioritize since the establishment of her business (line 16). This example also parallels Kellie's field notes about going to the drugstore with Magda to buy cards for both her customers and employees.

With regard to her employees, Magda has always rewarded them both symbolically and financially with presents during holidays. For example, all employees receive a handwritten Christmas card, a Christmas bonus and a bottle of champagne to commemorate the New Year. For Easter, employees receive large boxes of chocolate to share with their families. Additionally, Magda knows employees' birthdays and other important dates of their families in which cards and small presents are offered. Magda also buys every employee a small trinket when she travels. On one occasion when Magda visited Kellie abroad in Switzerland, Magda bought each of her employees a small souvenir and a box of chocolates. While these gestures appear small, they are significant to both Magda and her employees when it comes to nurturing and maintaining the social skills necessary for a leader within a small private business. Such gestures for Magda (and possibly her staff) index her appreciation of her staff without whom she would not have a business. Interestingly, features such as emotion, support, relationships and consideration are often associated with feminized cultural markers and are aspects of social skills and thus emotional intelligence (Galloway *et al.*, 2015), which we also associated with Magda as a business owner.

The social skills as well as the other components affiliated with Goleman's (2015) model of emotional intelligence are vital to Magda's leadership style within Shine. We contend that her ability to navigate her emotional intelligence, intercultural competence and her multilingual competence, together with her financial and management background, has allowed her business to thrive. While firing and hiring employees is part of any service business, Scott (2017: x) maintains that one of the most difficult but necessary parts of being a boss is 'telling people clearly and directly when their work isn't good enough'. Through our observations and interview data, we have witnessed Magda's diverse social skills in handling both rewarding and very challenging situations. Kellie remembers one specific and very uncomfortable situation when she was a teenager that had to do with a domestic worker who was accused of stealing by a customer. Magda needed to confront this employee and asked Kellie in advance if she would join the conversation and serve as a 'witness', to which Kellie agreed. Together in one room of Magda's house, Magda and her employee discussed the matter at length while Kellie stood in silence and listened. The domestic worker denied the accusations, and Magda believed her, which led to the cancellation of the home. Unfortunately, when this accusation occurred several months later with the same domestic worker albeit with a different customer, Magda called this domestic worker's former employer to discuss her behavior and work ethics, and found out that similar occurrences had also happened with her previous employer. Realizing that her domestic worker had stolen from two of her customers and blatantly lied to Magda, Magda fired her on the spot.

In one interview with Magda, she recalls the way in which she had to fire an employee who had been working for her for 12 years:

Extract (10)

1. Magda: not too long ago with [Maria] who erm worked here for 12 years, erm there was a
2.   complaint in a house, something about cleaning, nothing really, you know? But [Maria] was the
3.   type of person that erm, erm, she, she's right all the time, I mean, she's the only one who does it
4.   right and, and I had a meeting with her and she didn't let me speak, I, I couldn't speak, yeah, you
5.   know? And that had never really happened before and she was like very aggressive and erm…and
6.   so I said, 'Well, you know, you shouldn't work here anymore because it seems like you are not
7.   happy with me or with anybody else that you work with so'
8. Kellie: and she had been with you for 12 years?
9. Magda: 12 years, yeah

In recounting the scenario of firing a long-time employee, Magda discusses the interpersonal challenges, which inevitably led to this employee's termination. Interestingly enough, it was not the employee's satisfactory fulfillment of her cleaning duties that led to her termination, nor a customer's complaint, which Magda dismisses as minimal in 'nothing really, you know?' (line 2), but rather the employee's lack of interpersonal skills (lines 3–7). In this extract, Magda depicts her former employee as stubborn and aggressive. Such behavior may be interpreted as face threatening and, thus, questioning Magda's authority. In an attempt to remain calm and professional, Magda's clear and direct response (lines 6–7) ultimately did not leave any room for negotiation. Despite losing an employee who excelled at her work tasks, Magda's ability to sense her employee's dissatisfaction with her work, co-workers and Magda (lines 6 and 7) and empathize with it ultimately facilitated Magda's decision to terminate her employment at Shine. In this example, we witness Magda's power come to the fore and her authority as boss being played out with an employee, who is unable to communicate in a way that acknowledges this power asymmetry. This is perhaps one reason why Magda feels emboldened to remind her of her power by firing her on the spot. While Magda is indeed the boss of Shine, many of her communicative tasks include that of intercultural mediator, to which we now turn.

3.8 Mediation: The Case of Magda's Multilingual and Intercultural Competence

In this section, we focus on Magda as the owner and main operator of Shine, who serves as the main language broker and thus powerful mediator between her primarily Portuguese-speaking staff and English-speaking clients. To remind readers, Magda shares a migrant, Portuguese-speaking background with many of her employees; however, her university education, multilingual abilities and American citizenship serve as valuable symbolic resources that most of her employees lack.[1] As previously stated, the covert language policy of the company favors Portuguese, which reflects the majority language among her working-class Portuguese, Luso-Brazilian Portuguese and Spanish-speaking migrant female staff. Because of the multilingualism present within the company, Magda's brokering duties include 'inter-employee', in addition to employee-client brokering and mediation. Language policies are considered to be 'mechanisms of power' (Johnson & Ricento, 2013: 12); we argue that because of Magda's Brazilian background, emotional intelligence, cultural knowledge of European Portuguese, previous work experience and metalinguistic awareness, she is able to draw on her full linguistic repertoire or 'multi-competence' (Cook, 1991), which empower her brokering and mediating skills. Magda's cultural and linguistic capital may be her most important assets as an entrepreneur since they allow her to facilitate communication for the company's internal and external purposes while retaining the means of exercising power. Furthermore, Magda's ability to manipulate this kind of power through language and managerial strategies indexes her powerful (Vine, 2004) and at times demanding businesswoman identity while, simultaneously, contributing to her company's success.

3.8.1 Language brokering and facilitating communication between different parties

According to Tse (1996: 485) 'language brokers facilitate communication between two linguistically and/or culturally different parties. Unlike formal interpreters and translators, brokers mediate, rather than merely transmit, information'. Because language brokers are considered mediators and, often, decision-makers, they are equipped with metalinguistic awareness that is embedded within the ability to assess and act according to given situational contexts (Malakoff & Hakuta, 1991). Moreover, they tend to be very familiar with both parties' differing sociocultural perspectives. This knowledge allows brokers to tap into their sociocultural know-how to convey messages between parties by employing specific interpretive strategies, including adapting the message to suit the other party's sociocultural positioning. The majority of studies that look at language brokering, unlike the current study, have focused on children who serve as language brokers for their parents within various domains (Corona *et al.*, 2012; Del Torto, 2008; Jones & Trickett, 2005 [on cultural brokering]; Lazarevic *et al.*, 2014; Tse, 1995, 1996; Weisskirch, 2013) (although see the recent work of Söderlundh and Keevalik [2022] for a discussion of language brokering in a blue-collar workplace in Sweden).

3.8.2 Company-internal communication: Launch of a Portuguese-by-design cleaning company

Within the context of Magda's cleaning company, economic gain and symbolic capital are associated with the use of Portuguese. European Portuguese is the L1 of the majority of her employees. This demographic reflects Magda's bias toward Portuguese women, whose strong work ethic and honesty make them, according to Magda, model house cleaners. Although Portuguese is a minority language on both national and regional levels, it is endowed with linguistic authority on the local level because of its link to upward mobility within the cleaning company. In fact, Magda's conception of her company was strongly tied to her positive perception of Portuguese cleaners. An investigation into her hiring practices confirmed that, indeed, she primarily relies on local transcultural Portuguese networks for new employee referrals and that Portuguese workers make up the majority of her current staff (see Figure 3.1). At the time of our investigation into Magda's company in 2011, she had a total of 19 employees: 18 domestic workers (two of whom also served as drivers) and one driver who did not clean houses.

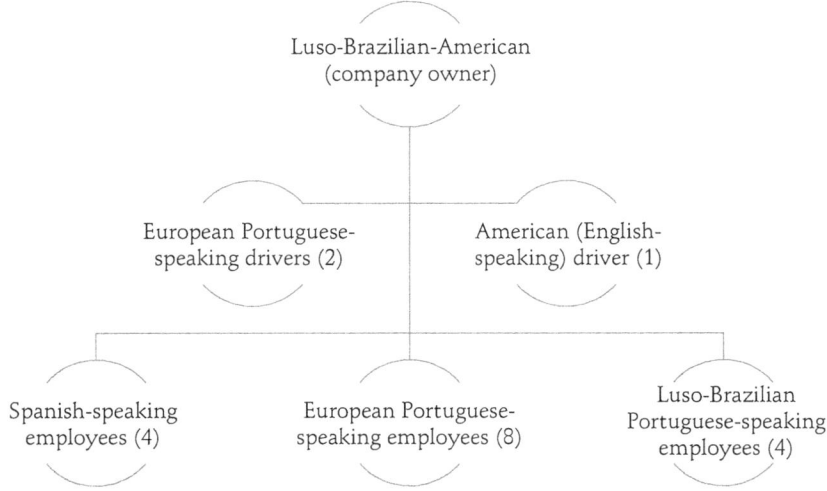

Figure 3.1 The cleaning company hierarchy: Magda is at the top of the hierarchy, where company values and job instructions trickle down to her employees. Of the four Spanish-speaking employees, three are from Ecuador and one is from Honduras

The company's majority European Portuguese-speaking workforce (as indicated in Figure 3.1) reflects Magda's expressed preference for these employees. Magda, an L1 Luso-Brazilian Portuguese speaker herself, employs four Brazilians. The covert, company-internal language policy that favors Portuguese comes out of these numbers. Furthermore, our observations of casual interactions between co-workers suggested that Portuguese is also connected to feelings of 'sisterhood' (Goldstein, 1997) between employees. Some knowledge of Portuguese would, thus, benefit all employees as it functioned as a soft skill within the company (Urciuoli, 2008).

3.8.3 Magda's preference for Portuguese employees

The factors contributing to Magda's preference for employing Portuguese as the company-internal language have to do with her own L1, but, more importantly, with her visions of the company's philosophy. As stated previously, she strongly values the Portuguese work ethic and has created a company that reflects this bias. Moreover, as indicated by Extract (11), Magda also values Portuguese women's ability to comply with orders.

Extract (11)

1.	Anne:	yeah erm, would you ever consider hiring like, do you think it would work out if you employed
2.		an English speaker who didn't speak Portuguese or Spanish?
3.	Magda:	honestly? …they don't wanna work, they don't want to… it would be unaccept,
4.		unacceptable? Erm for them, they would think that we work too hard, I mean I'm very
5.		demanding and erm I think working with the Portuguese erm actually I like to work with the
6.		Portuguese better than erm with the Brazilians erm you know, whatever I tell them to do,
7.		they are you know? more accept, they accept it better, the, the Brazilians are 'Oh, do I have
8.		to do this' 'Yes, you do' and erm I always say to them if, if I hire a Brazilian you know and I
9.		have a few Brazilians and they are really very nice but when I hire them I say, 'Listen, if
10.		you have any problems with one of my Portuguese employees, if somebody's gonna go
11.		home, it's gonna be you, it's not gonna be the Portuguese girl'.

In this extract, Magda expresses strong favoritism toward Portuguese workers because she believes in their superior capacity to carry out the company's mission. This favoritism is contrasted with Magda's negative characterizations of the local English-speaking population and the Brazilians' difficulty in accepting authority. Magda employs two stance markers, *actually* (line 5) and *honestly* (line 3), which signal her attitude about employees with different L1s. Her use of *honestly* expresses her opinion about potential English-speaking employees and their inability to fit into the company for several reasons, including, primarily, their differing ideas about work that are rooted in their American upbringing. The directness of *actually, honestly* and *listen* (line 9) suggests a stance that is uninfluenced by politeness strategies and, as such, reflective of Magda's higher position in the workplace hierarchy. Her demeanor as an employer reinforces this stance: it is acceptable for a manager to be 'very demanding' (lines 4 and 5) but not an employee. These features index her authoritative, agentive voice because she can change the demand to suit her preference. These workers' easy acceptance of instructions (line 7) is a product of their submissive roles within the company hierarchy. In subsequent statements, Magda connects this role with her employees' gender: they are submissive because they have to serve their Portuguese husbands at home. Her company provides another context for them to carry out their traditional gender roles.[2]

The Portuguese staff is contrasted with the Brazilian staff, who 'work well and are very nice' (line 9), but may question her instructions (line 7). Her use of the interjection 'oh' within the direct reported speech clause is a performative that conveys her negative opinion of their reaction (Carter & McCarthy, 2006: 224) to her instructions, which she interprets as a challenge to her authority and, quite possibly, a face-threatening act (Brown & Levinson, 1987; Vine, 2009). Magda's use of on-the-record directness to describe her response to these perceived challenges is on display with her use of another direct reported speech clause: 'Yes, you do [have to do it]'. Furthermore, Magda reaffirms her powerful position as the person responsible for her workers' employment status by issuing a forceful warning (lines 10 and 11).

3.8.4 Explicit choices: Portuguese as the covert company language

Magda's preference for Portuguese working values (as discussed in the previous section) was also voiced by more than one of the Spanish-speaking employees. Lila from Ecuador, who is married to a Portuguese man, cites this preference as a reason for working with this Portuguese-speaking cleaning company instead of a Spanish-speaking one:

Extract (12)

    1. Lila: *pero no me gusta trabajar con hispanos* (but I don't like to work with [Spanish speakers])
    2. Anne: *por qué?* (why?)

3. Lila: *porque… cuando viene a otro [de nuestro país] no te tratan de ayudar… ellos son muy*
4. *egoísta, me entienden?* (because, when another person comes [from our country], they don't try to help you, they are very self-centered, you understand?)
5. Lila: *cualquier hispano…entonces es preferible trabajar con otras personas que con ellos…nunca*
6. *te tratan de ayudar, Son egoístas. No puedes pedir un favor decirles 'me enseñas eso'. No*
7. *quieren. En cambio si tú te vas al portugués o cualquier otro, te enseña es más sociable* (whichever [Spanish speaker] …it's preferable to work with people other than them…they never try and help you. They are selfish. You can't ask for a favor and say 'teach me this'. They don't want to. In contrast, if you go to a Portuguese person or whoever else, they'll teach you. They're more sociable).

The same employees who Magda views favorably for their submissive nature and superior capacity to accept instructions are considered much more sociable and helpful by Lila than people with her own language background (line 1). In discussing previous employment experiences with local Spanish speakers Lila, too, expresses her opinion through generalizations: she considers Spanish speakers (from Central and South America), regardless of their country of origin, to be 'not helpful' and 'selfish' (line 4). As a result, she, too, prefers to work with the Portuguese. Interestingly, Lila's preferences parallel those of Magda in that she too prefers working with (European) Portuguese speakers. This example thus highlights some traits of the company culture discussed by Magda.

Although Lila could use Spanish to communicate with many of her Portuguese-speaking co-workers (who claim to understand Spanish), we found that she, instead, draws on her truncated multilingual repertoire (Blommaert, 2010) and infuses some Portuguese lexical items into her Spanish-language speech. By incorporating some Portuguese into her speech, Lila invests in Portuguese as a symbolic resource. These practices, along with her interview comments, reflect her orientation toward Portuguese. Interviews with the other Spanish-speaking employees suggest that they, too, make efforts to adapt in a similar direction. This topic receives much more detailed examination in Chapter 4, which takes a deep dive into the dynamics of interaction between Shine's Spanish-speaking employees and the Lusophone employees who have not developed many accommodation or Spanish-language skills.

3.8.5 Mediating between different language varieties via 'inter-employee brokering'

Despite the Spanish-speaking employees' efforts to adapt to the company's covert Portuguese language policy, misunderstandings between co-workers still occur. This is also true for communication between Portuguese and Brazilian employees as Extract (13) suggests. Primarily in an effort to help non-European Portuguese speakers navigate this European Portuguese-centric company, we found that Magda, at times, engages in what we call 'inter-employee' brokering and mediation:

Extract (13)

1. Magda: Mara is from Brazil. [...]Mara is married to a Portuguese guy, so she...understands
2. that kind of language...if I had a brand new Brazilian that had not had, you know, too much
3. contact with Portuguese people, erm it would be you know, erm difficult. But what I say to
4. them is like you know, you have to understand that Portuguese people say some things that
5. means differently. You know, it may sound like erm insulting to us to Brazilians but it's, it's
6. not you know? [...]There are a lot words, a lot of reactions from you know from Portuguese
7. that are different from the Brazilians but erm, erm if you really understand it's just the way
8. they express themselves, they don't mean that, a Brazilian has to understand that, I do and if
9. sometimes...someone complains about this, I explain it to them.

In this extract, Magda provides an example in which she must tap into her cultural and metalinguistic awareness in order to mediate between employees who speak different L1 varieties. She references a current Brazilian employee who is married to a Portuguese man and, therefore, 'understands that kind of language' (lines 1 and 2). Her comments suggest that European Portuguese differs considerably from Luso-Brazilian Portuguese and that mutual intelligibility cannot be assumed.[3] Due to Magda's familiarity with European Portuguese (lines 4–9), she is able to draw on her 'multicompetence' and 'active repertoire' (Matras, 2009) for communicative goals to be met within particular scenarios of language contact such as this one in which Brazilians may otherwise be insulted.

We claim that engaging in 'inter-employee brokering' imbues Magda with further symbolic power by drawing on the linguistic and cultural capital necessary for smooth and harmonious interactions between co-workers, who speak different varieties of Portuguese. In essence, Magda can serve as the source of information that, at times, plays a valuable role in facilitating co-workers' communication.

Magda's familiarity with Spanish, too, serves as a resource for her Spanish-speaking employees as indicated in Extract (14):

Extract (14)

1. Anne: do you normally choose Spanish or do you normally choose Portuguese [to address a group
2. of workers]?
3. Magda: if I do a memo you know, I will write it in Portuguese, yeah and I tell the girls in Spanish, 'If
4. you don't understand, you know just ask me' but they will receive the memo in Portuguese
5. also.

The above extract provides insight into Magda's unwritten rules for clarification and further evidence that Portuguese is the company's default language. Magda's translation and inter-employee brokering serve an important function within the company. However, as Lila's comments in Extract (12) suggest, the employees themselves also negotiate communication with their co-workers. The nature of this accommodation appears to be bidirectional: we found examples of both Spanish speakers accommodating to Portuguese speakers as well as Portuguese speakers accommodating to Spanish speakers. The direction of accommodation appears to depend largely on the language repertoires and resourcefulness of the specific speakers involved. Of the employees who make little effort to accommodate to their co-workers, all are Portuguese. The company's language policy favors them and creates less incentive for them to expand their language repertoires.[4]

3.8.6 Language brokering and Magda's authority over employees

Similar to their efforts to accommodate to co-workers from Luso-Brazilian or Spanish-speaking backgrounds, this sub-group of Portuguese workers shows a limited ability to accommodate to their English-speaking clients. As Magda explains in Extract (15), her language brokering between clients and employees removes much of the potential communication difficulties:

Extract (15)

1. Magda: If they [the customers] leave a note, erm [one of the cleaning ladies] will pick up the erm
2. phone and say 'Well you know, I understand so much, so much but there's this that I don't
3. understand' depending where it is you know sometimes I say, 'Well, spell it for me' you know? and

4.	she starts spelling and I can just you know pick up right away 'Oh ok, that's it' so I will give her the
5.	instructions, yeah

Magda functions as the company's disseminator of instructions both during the initial planning process as well as in cases of spontaneous changes/clarifications that cannot be communicated directly between the customer and the worker. Magda's micromanagement diminishes employees' need for English language proficiency while enhancing her legitimated domination over them. Furthermore, the workers' reliance on Magda influences their perception of the important skills for the job:

Extract (16)

1.	Paloma:	... *As vezes a gente quer se falar mais coisas ou as mulheres às vezes querem nos falar a*
2.		*nós a gente não consegue (.) a gente pronto a gente hello, good morning ou bye-bye ou assim mas*
3.		*(.) o essencial mesmo não sabe e, quer e não consegue e (.) mas pronto, mas a gente pra mim acho*
4.		*que se a gente, souber falar o essencial por exemplo, hello, good morning, o mais importante, ser*
5.		*simpático pra mulheres pra falar (.) pronto o essencial, de ser educado assim* (because, well, because sometimes we want to be able to say more things or the women sometimes would like to say more to us and we aren't able to (.) we well we hello, good morning or bye-bye like that but (.) the important things really we don't know it's, you want to but you're not able to, but anyway, we for me I think if we're able to say the essentials for example, hello, good morning. The most important thing, is to speak nicely to the women (.) well the most important thing is to be polite)

In this extract, Paloma, a European Portuguese-speaking domestic, explains that she does not possess the linguistic capital necessary for her to work as an independent housecleaner (line 3). However, the explanation that follows this statement minimizes the importance of English for her job: being nice, respectful and polite to the clients surpasses the need to converse with them (line 5). When more elaborate communication is required, Paloma simply calls Magda and relies on her to do the brokering work as stated later in Paloma's interview. Paloma's truncated multilingual repertoire and limited English proficiency are thus 'in sync' with a working context in which Magda is always available for consultation.

Magda's language brokering also intensifies her contact with clients. Due in part to this more intense contact, employees believe that Magda may pass by a customer's house at any moment to check in with them and to judge the quality of her employees' work. The possibility of this occurring, according to one long-time employee, Bianca, is ever-present and stressful:

Extract (17)

1. Bianca: *[Magda] quer tudo muito bem feito, e quando chega nas casas, nós sempre trememos um*
2. *pouquinho...apesar dos anos que nós trabalhamos com ela...porque não sei porque... precisamente*
3. *no sítio onde eu esqueci de limpar hoje é que a Magda vai lá passar a mão ou um pano...*

Bianca: [Magda] wants everything to be done well, and when she arrives at the houses, we always tremble a little bit...despite all of the years we've been working with her...because I don't know why...in exactly the place where I forgot to clean today it might be that Magda goes there and runs her hand or a cloth over it...

In Extract (17), Bianca describes Magda's way of holding her employees accountable for their work. Magda's position as a language broker increases her direct interaction with customers and the opportunities to inspect her employees' work. Her employees are keenly aware of this possibility. Her language brokering activities are thus tied to her authority over her employees and to her presentation of herself as the legitimate speaker for the company in the company's external communications. In the preceding examples, power is tied to the linguistic and material resources required in worker-customer interactions. As Magda is able to supply the language necessary to facilitate these interactions, she gains greater power and legitimated domination over employees.

3.9 Company-External Communication: A Language Policy for Customers

Magda's micromanagement style is also reflected in the language policy designed for communication between customers and workers. In Extract (18), Magda briefly describes this policy:

Extract (18)

1. Kellie: do you give them [the clients] explicit instructions...not to communicate with the cleaning
2. ladies or?
3. Magda: no... I don't tell them, 'don't communicate', there, there is erm, erm, a paragraph [in the

4.	company's information booklet] that says, 'Do not leave a note because most of the cleaning ladies
5.	do not speak English' so they may not understand and we really want to do a good job...if you leave
6.	a note, you leave it to me so then I can you know, tell the cleaning lady this, this and that and erm
7.	you know, there's no miscommunication in there [....] I tell some customers, 'If you leave a note for
8.	her, she's gonna take that note for me, so if you're asking her to do something, it may not get done'
9.	[...] I mean the customers are told not to leave a note...but, but if they leave a note and some of
10.	them don't follow the rules you know?

This extract refers to the seven-page document intended for clients that conveys details about the company's service and their expectations for customers. We checked this document and, indeed, this explicit request appears on page one in bold italics: *'Please do not leave any notes for the cleaning lady, as many do not speak English fluently'*.

This extract helps to show the role of language brokering in preserving a top-down communication structure in which Magda leaves very little room for horizontal or bottom-up input. As the company owner and primary language broker between her clients and employees, Magda is not only able to oversee any communication between the two groups, but she attempts to maintain full control over it. This becomes apparent through the changes in pronoun use from the inclusive 'we' to the use of the singular first-person pronoun 'I' (lines 5 and 6), suggesting that, initially, the company [the group of women] wants to do a good job, but in order for this to occur, Magda [the individual] requires instructions or requests from customers directly (lines 6 and 9). Magda positions herself as the individual with the power to change her employees' practice: Magda – rather than the clients – disseminates instructions to the domestics, and they carry out their cleaning duties according to her instructions. This kind of employee micromanagement, which was done via brokering, occurred repeatedly throughout our time with Magda.[5]

Furthermore, Magda's use of imperatives demonstrates, once again, a very direct, on-the-record speaking style that helps to indicate her position of power. In line 4, the imperative 'do not leave a note' also functions as a possible warning or repercussion, and, as such, references Magda's agentive voice through her ability to influence this repercussion. Again, these are Magda's rules (line 10), and failure to comply with them has a consequence, which, in this case, is a less-than-optimal cleaning job due solely to clients' inability to follow Magda's explicit instructions rather than her employees' inability to read and understand notes written in

English. While clients may accuse Magda's employees for other reasons, possessing 'scant material resources' (Duchêne *et al.*, 2013: 7) based on their English skills (or lack thereof) is not accepted by Magda and illustrates a way in which language operates as a means of social control within this local context.

Overall, we found that Magda's brokering duties between her employees and clients, along with the explicit language policy that customers are supposed to adhere to, assist Magda's micromanagement of her employees and maintenance of control over the cleaning and business operations.

3.9.1 Power relations between Magda and her customers

As the company's policy against clients' leaving notes for the cleaning staff suggests, Magda's transfer of symbolic and material resources into her powerful position extends beyond company-internal communication. Throughout our discussions with Magda, it became clear that she makes many specific choices about company operations and company size, which over the years has alternated according to her personal preferences rather than market forces.

As with any small business, Magda's company relies on the market forces that create demand for her professional cleaning services. This demand is high in the local context and places Magda in the powerful position of selecting the clients that suit her. The upsurge in middle-class women entering the workforce over the last few decades likely contributes to this demand (Anderson, 2001). In this way, macro-level market dynamics of the new market appear to influence this micro-level situation. One customer's awareness of this selectivity comes through in the extract below:

Extract (19)

1. Mrs Gloski: I felt that Magda, erm, was very helpful to me because she knew in the past that I was
2. using her on a temporary basis and I needed the help, I'm also erm coming out of chemotherapy so
3. erm, it was – I was anxious to have them work erm have them...

With her descriptions of Magda's helpfulness and friendliness, Mrs Gloski appears to re-conceptualize traditional customer-worker relations. In this case, Magda's acceptance of Mrs Gloski as a customer is constructed as a helpful act during a very difficult time in her life rather than a pure business agreement. In a later portion of the interview, Mrs Gloski provides a practical reason that supported her bid for acceptance as a customer:

Extract (20)

    1. Mrs Gloski: I also know that this, erm particular space is easy to mani– easier to maneuver
    2. because it's, fairly spare…as compared to [my neighbor's] who has a lot more stuff going on…so, I
    3. just felt, at ease.

Mrs Gloski classifies the burden on the cleaning staff of cleaning her apartment as minimal. She understands that Magda does not accept everyone as a client; however, her uncluttered apartment and her infirmity provided compelling reasons to 'help her'. Instead of the company being helped by the income from paying customers, customers like Mrs Gloski appear to view the situation in reverse. In these ways, this example relates directly to our discussion about supply and demand addressed earlier in the chapter and Magda's ability to choose her clients.

Through our interview with Magda, we learned that adding Mrs Gloski to her list of clients, in fact, was a decidedly straightforward process that was based primarily on logistics. First, Mrs Gloski, as a referral from one of Magda's existing clients, was adhering to Magda's referral rule for initiating services. Second, Mrs Gloski's residence in the same apartment complex as the client who referred her served to minimize logistical work: the clients' proximity to one another allowed Magda to take on an additional client without disturbing the employee transfer system that was already in place. Magda pointed to this practical consideration as an important factor that influenced her decision to accept Mrs Gloski as a client.[6] In these ways, Magda is constructed as the chief decision-maker who is in control of the clientele she accepts. Moreover, her client appears to recognize the business's selectivity and expresses her gratitude for being selected although she is the paying customer.

The above example is contrasted with that of a client's husband who neither recognizes Magda's position of power nor expresses gratitude (or even respect) for the cleaning service.

The following extract begins with Magda's description of a telephone conversation with a client's husband who called to inquire about the location of a missing puzzle piece from the children's playroom:

Extract (21)

    1. Magda: I said, 'Well, I think it's going to be impossible' a piece of puzzle that my cleaning lady? He said
    2. to me, 'oh, I don't know where you find these people, they have no brains', I have never been rude,
    3. but I said, 'you know what, since you have the brains, from now on you clean your house' and I hung

4.	up the phone. Two seconds later, his wife called me and she said, 'Magda, please, do not cancel my
5.	house, my husband had a bad day at work today and he's very upset', I said, 'I have nothing to do with
6.	the, the bad day he had at work and he should be respectful to my cleaning ladies and also to myself,
7.	I'm canceling your house, find somebody else'. Three weeks later, she calls me and she said, 'Magda,
8.	could you please come back, please, please'. I said, 'no, once I cancel a house, it's done'. Three months
9.	later, she called me and she said, 'we have had like six companies to clean our house, nobody ever
10.	cleaned our house the way you guys clean, please come back, I can give you anything you want'. I said,
11.	'if you pay me a thousand dollars a week, I would not clean your house, thank you, but no thank you',
12.	the end.

Magda's negative assessment about finding the missing puzzle piece is taken up by the husband in which he blatantly accuses Magda of being a poor employer and the cleaning ladies as having 'no brains' (line 2). These insults are interpreted by Magda as face-threatening and function to justify her 'rude' response and behavior (lines 3 and 4). The linguistic strategies and actions employed throughout the extract index the asymmetrical relations of power between Magda and her clients within this context. Although the husband assumes power in his initial conversation with Magda, Magda quickly reverses the power dynamics by cancelling his house. She leaves the wife in a powerless position in which she makes repeated requests that Magda refuses to grant.

Because Magda is in the professional service sector, customers are usually regarded as those who provide the material resources in exchange for symbolic ones. The client, therefore, may be considered as retaining the power-over their service provider. According to Magda's account, this client's power was immediately usurped by her agentive actions. With her decision to cancel the house, Magda reinstituted herself as not only the authoritative figure within her company, but, simultaneously, the legitimate spokesperson for the company. Not only does Magda refuse to tolerate disrespect when it is aimed at her, she does not accept it when it is directed at her employees (lines 6–7). Despite numerous calls from the wife over time, who is positioned as both desperate and apologetic (line 8), Magda retains full control of the situation. Magda's refusal to grant these customers their request and their inability to alter the situation illustrates her agentive voice.

Magda further demonstrates her unwillingness to tolerate a client's disrespectful behavior through her refusal to accept increased monetary compensation. The reported speech clause in line 7 is done through the means of a forceful directive, 'I'm cancelling your house, find somebody else', which further positions Magda as a powerful businesswoman who places more value on her employees and their services than potential economic gain. Based on our ethnographic data and conversations with Magda, we found that Magda only cancels customers' homes for two main reasons: their failure to pay on time or their disrespectful behavior to either her employees or her.[7] This extract illustrates that Magda's brokering duties between clients and domestics extend beyond the pure transmission of information; they also function as a means of maintaining power relations between the company and its clients.

This finding, together with the previous discussion that reinforces Magda's position at the top of the company hierarchy, helps to paint Magda as an agentive company owner who employs various communicative strategies to maintain her position of power in customer-employee, employer-employee, and customer-company owner relations.

3.10 Chapter Summary

In this chapter, we have provided readers with both ethnographic and biographical details of Magda in order for readers to gain better insight into Magda's own transnational journey from Brazil to the US to work for a family as a live-in nanny and, thus, domestic worker herself in the 1970s. The experiences and challenges Magda had as a child and young adult have had an impact on her as a person as well as her emotional intelligence, which we claim has helped to shape Magda's approach as a female, migrant entrepreneur and business owner of Shine. By exploring Goleman's (2000, 2015) model of emotional intelligence – which consists of self-awareness, self-regulation, motivation, empathy and social skills – we wanted to underscore Magda's 'softer side' as an individual and employer, who simultaneously has a no-nonsense business leadership style. As such, the aim of the chapter was to illuminate Magda's multifaceted identities as a female, migrant business owner by tracing both her personal and professional identities in order to provide a deeper and more nuanced picture of Magda overall. She is at once empathetic while simultaneously being a 'demanding' employer.

The second half of the chapter took a closer look into Shine and the ways in which communication functions in order for Shine to run smoothly. Due to Magda's intercultural, multilingual and, thus, communicative competence in different Portuguese varieties as well as her ability to understand, speak and use Spanish with employees when necessary, one of Magda's main functions at Shine is to serve as its company's primary language broker when mediating between individuals. This mediation occurred among employees who speak different varieties and/or languages, a concept we have termed 'inter-employee brokering', as well as for company external purposes between Magda's employees and her primarily English-speaking clients. We have claimed that both Magda's emotional intelligence as well as her brokering abilities, coupled with her financial and managerial background, are major assets to her as a successful business owner. Similarly, we provided examples to show how Magda's language brokering duties put her in a very powerful position relative to her employees, allowing her to micromanage, and, in this way, control communication between her employees and customers. At the same time, this brokering allows Magda to tap into a surplus pool of female migrant employees who need to work but do not speak English. In fact, speaking English at Shine for potential and current employees is not a requirement for recruitment purposes, a finding that is not in line with contemporary language and workplace studies that assume employees must speak the language of the host community for reasons of employability and or social mobility to occur within a company's hierarchy. As we discussed, European Portuguese rather than English was the language imbued with the most symbolic power within this local workplace context. It is this finding which questions the existing literature on multilingual workplaces and the political economy of language that for quite some time has found and regarded English (and or the language of the state depending on the context) to carry the most symbolic capital. With Shine, this was not the case. This topic receives more detailed attention in chapter five, which addresses employees' communicative multicompetence despite self-reported low levels of English-language proficiency. In the next chapter, we discuss Shine's and the larger Ironbound community's Portuguese-language abilities.

Notes

(1) At the time of data collection, only one of Magda's employees had a university degree.
(2) This claim was confirmed by the 10 European Portuguese (EP) women who were all married with children. This finding is in line with what Hochschild (1989) has termed 'the traditional woman' and 'the second shift'. Hochschild found that working-class women and men preferred women to take on traditional gender roles within labor performed at home in addition to paid labor outside the home context.
(3) The literature does not regard European (EP) and Luso-Brazilian Portuguese (LBP) as two monolithic categories. Rather, regional dialects exist within each variety. The more simplistic distinction between EP and LBP in the current discussion is tied to intelligibility. Magda's Portuguese employees speak different – albeit mutually intelligible – EP varieties (as confirmed in our interviews). Greater differences exist between spoken EP and LBP varieties. As vowel reduction across the EP varieties is more extreme than in LBP varieties, phonological differences between them represent the most striking challenge to mutual intelligibility (Azevedo, 2005). Lexical, morpho-syntactic and metapragmatic differences between EP and LBP may also lead to miscommunication between speakers of EP and LBP (as Magda and her employees explain in their interviews.).

(4) From our interviews and observations, we also found that some employees from different L1 backgrounds engaged in 'dual-linguality' (Piller, 2002: 24–25) or receptive bilingualism in which each speaker uses her L1 to communicate with the other. Dualinguality receives more attention with respect to Hispanophone and Lusophone employees' communication in Chapter 4.
(5) In the evenings, Magda is occupied with speaking to clients directly on the phone and taking notes of their requests. Magda then relays these requests or instructions to her employees before they arrive at the clients' houses.
(6) Each employee is assigned to one house during the morning shift. The afternoon shift is shorter but includes two employees per house. Drivers are responsible for transporting and transferring employees throughout the day. Since clients' homes are distributed between several towns, transfers can take up to 20 minutes. Clients' close proximity to one another is favorable to Magda since it allows her drivers to transfer workers more efficiently.
(7) Magda has in the past cancelled customers' homes due to late payments but also if employees were wrongly accused of breaking items or stealing. In the latter case, Magda explained that cancelling a home is the best option for her company since employees no longer feel comfortable in a client's home, where their trust has been questioned. Cancelling a house can be initially difficult for Magda, her employees and the clients, but over the years, Magda's business has not suffered economically since the demand for her services remains very high. Therefore, whenever a house is cancelled, a vacancy to clean a new home becomes available, and, according to Magda and her employees, this vacancy is filled within the same week.

4 The Interplay between Identity, Ideology and Capital that Strengthens Cultural Attachments: The Pull of Portuguese and the Portuguese-Centric Ironbound Community for Shine's Hispanophone Employees

4.1 Introduction

Thus far in this book, we have drawn attention to Shine's Portuguese-centric company culture and image, both of which stem from Magda's founding visions for her business. These areas of focus have contributed to a portrait of a successful migrant business that employs workers with a wide range of English-language resources. Despite Shine's Anglophone clientele and English-dominant setting, its smooth operation – as discussed in the previous chapter – relies far less on its employees' English-language competence than their Portuguese-language abilities. Employment in such a company represents an understandable choice for its Lusophone workers; however, this choice is less clear-cut for its Hispanophone Latino workers, who could potentially seek employment at one of the numerous Hispanophone-dominant cleaning companies in the greater Newark area. What drives this choice? What are some of the dynamics that make this choice a viable option?

These questions guide the discussion to which this chapter now turns. They bring into focus an example of *horizontal assimilation*, the act of strongly affiliating with the culture of a non-dominant group that is different from one's own (Prashad, 2001). As this setting values

Portuguese-language proficiency, it informs an inquiry that reassesses the influence of *decapitalization* (Martín Rojo, 2013; Moyer, 2018), the process through which linguistic capital diminishes as a result of a shift in a language's status from dominant to minority. In this case, the analysis addresses the extent to which the notion of decapitalization applies to Portuguese as a migrant language in the Newark area. With these areas of emphasis, the current chapter moves away from the preceding chapter's focus on Magda and shifts it onto her employees. It gives the most attention to the company's Hispanophone employees by addressing interview data that come from three members of this four-person group.

The ensuing exploration weaves these voices into a larger discussion about neoliberal capital flows, migration and belonging. Participants' orientations are intricately tied to the three primary tenets of investment: capital (Section 4.5) identity (Section 4.7) and ideology (Section 4.8) (Darvin & Norton, 2015). This model of investment envisions each of these components as intertwined with one another: capital influences ideologies toward languages and cultures, and these ideologies largely account for participants' identification (or lack thereof) with them. For a fuller description of this model, see Darvin and Norton (2015). Analysis that focuses on these three aspects of investment, thus, helps to contextualize and account for the orientation of Shine's Hispanophone Latinas to the Newark-area Lusophone community. While positive ideologies toward heritage language(s) and culture(s) exist across diaspora groups, the introduction of capital into this system, as suggested by the data analyzed below, fortifies these ideologies and potentially extends them to other local diaspora groups. Capital plays an essential role within this system, and, accordingly, receives considerable attention in this chapter. As it represents one of the three inter-related components of investment, however, it appears here as part of a larger discussion about the interplay between ideology, identity and capital as they relate to the Portuguese-centric community of greater Newark, New Jersey.

For these reasons, the sections below provide a more detailed description of these strands and their connections to one another. A brief comparison of Portuguese vs. Spanish phonology following this section provides additional context for this chapter's analysis, and the subsequent section on capital, neoliberalism and the Portuguese-centric diaspora applies some of the key concepts and trends from the literature to the local setting. With this background and understanding of the setting in mind, the chapter then turns to its primary analysis, which addresses Hispanophone employees' accommodation strategies within Shine and, in a later section, their orientations to Portuguese-centric communities beyond Shine.

4.2 The Shifting Dynamics of Capital and Migration: The Conditions for Emergent Cultural-Linguistic Orientations toward Non-Dominant Groups

Freer flows of capital under neoliberalism have given rise to alternatives to the dominant culture's marketplace and have provided new spaces for migrants to participate in the mainstream economy (Sabaté i Dalmau, 2013). The considerable revenue generated from these businesses grants them legitimacy as sites that accumulate capital. In this way, the valuation of linguistic capital has shifted (DeCosta, 2010), giving rise to new conceptualizations of identity, citizenship and belonging (Darvin, 2016; Lim *et al.*, 2018; Warriner, 2007; Williams *et al.*, 2022). These considerations are fundamental to understanding the pull of the market associated with the Newark-based Portuguese-centric community as a viable alternative to both the market of each Hispanophone participant's own diasporic community and that of the dominant culture.

The capital that is associated with a language has long been correlated with its appeal to potential learners (Magro, 2016). For the purposes of this discussion, the analysis draws on Bourdieu's (1986) distinction between cultural, economic and social capital. Traditionally, for migrant communities, acquisition of the adopted country's dominant language has held the most symbolic power because of its economic capital. Moreover, through its ability to grant access to local educational opportunities and social networks, the host language has also traditionally been a source of cultural and social capital. In contrast, the languages that migrants have brought with them to their adopted communities have traditionally lost value as they have been judged according to the prejudices and expectations of the new local setting, or, as referred to by Blommaert (2010), the new *orders of indexicality* that are present in the receiving country. In Bourdieu's (1986) terms, they lose their economic capital in the new context and, to varying degrees according to the specific dynamics of the local setting, their cultural and social capital as well. The term 'decapitalization', thus, refers to the devaluation of a migrant's linguistic capital in school (Martín Rojo, 2013) and work contexts (Moyer, 2018). Indeed, this devaluation of linguistic capital mirrors the trend of migrants' lower return on their human capital that results from diminished employment prospects within the general labor market (i.e. non-ethnic economies) (Light *et al.*, 1994).

With its focus on capital, this chapter re-examines such themes as 'decapitalization' with respect to the lived experiences and language choices of Shine's Hispanophone employees and finds that this process cannot be assumed for all contexts, including the one presented here.

This counterevidence comes from a small number of studies that highlight participants' orientation toward another local migrant group. Through its appeal to those who share a marginalized orientation, the variety associated with this group gains cultural capital. This is the case for European Spanish artists' appropriation of less prestigious Latin American varieties in Spanish-language hip hop (Magro, 2016), non-Turkish migrant youths' co-opting of Turkish lexicon in Germany (Dirim & Auer, 2012), and non-Moroccan migrants' use of Moroccan-accented Dutch to show their affiliation with their Moroccan counterparts in the Netherlands (Nortier & Dorleijn, 2008).

Such examples show acquisition attempts that are restricted to certain domains and features; more comprehensive examples of acquisition have received limited attention in workplace contexts. Among North America-based, white-collar businesses not owned by migrants that employ staff from different diaspora groups, inter-diasporic communication typically relies on a combination of English and multimodality (Kleifgen, 2013), an aspect of communication that, as detailed in Chapter 5, also features prominently in Shine's employee-customer interactions. Within blue-collar sectors dominated by members of one diaspora group that demonstrates minimal English-language competence, the picture is different: similarly to Shine, the variety of the most prominent migrant group typically serves as the primary means of inter-diasporic communication, fostering solidarity between co-workers across ethno-linguistic divides (Goldstein, 1997). Within informal sectors, acquiring the language of the migrant group that dominates the sector grants greater access to this network (Vigouroux, 2013).

Indeed, participation in the ethnic economy provides a revenue-generating alternative to employment within the so-called general labor market. The extent to which participation in the ethnic vs. general labor market influences workers' wage-earning potential has long represented the subject of debate within the literature (Light *et al.*, 1994); nevertheless, it is clear that employment in migrant-owned businesses, at the very least, mitigates the effects of decapitalization with respect to the primary language of inter-employee communication when the owner and the employees share a common language.

In the case of Shine's Hispanophone employees, engagement with another locally prominent migrant group extends beyond the workplace domain. The analysis that follows uses the theoretical lenses of Communication Accommodation Theory (Bourhis, 1991; Stell & Dragojevic, 2017), community of practice (Lave & Wenger, 1991; Wenger, 1998) and investment (Darvin & Norton, 2015; Norton, 2000, 2013) to outline the magnitude and means through which the extended Ironbound community – together with its languages and cultures – assert local influence alongside the regionally dominant language (English) and culture

(American). With this focus, it re-examines the notion of decapitalization with respect to the cultural, social and economic capital associated with Portuguese in the local context.

Through its profiling of a capital-rich alternative to the dominant language and culture, the discussion below responds to Vigouroux's (2013: 243) call to 'investigate the issue of socioeconomic integration without preconceived social categories (e.g. *locals* versus *migrants*) to whom it may apply'. It, thus, moves beyond underlying assumptions that migrants need to adapt to the dominant language and culture in order to gain a foothold within their adopted community. The ways in which Portuguese-language knowledge allows Shine's Hispanophone employees to access opportunities represents the primary topic of inquiry.

4.3 An Introduction to this Chapter's Primary Participants

In this chapter, our analysis focuses on extracts from interviews with four participants: one Portuguese (Dona Aura), one Honduran (Anita) and two Ecuadorian (Lila and Nina) employees. Dona Aura, a 55-year-old Portuguese employee of Shine for nine years who has resided in the US for 13 years, is an established figure at Shine. Although she started working at Shine after its founding, she blends in with the founding core group through her age, Portuguese origins and years of experience. Her co-workers' use of the address term *Dona* (Mrs) in front of her first name demonstrates respect for her age and experience. The three Hispanophone employees profiled here have a relatively junior status within the company. Anita is a 25-year-old employee from Honduras who has been in the US for six years and has been working at Shine for approximately four of these years. Lila, a 26-year-old employee from Ecuador who has been living in the US for five years and working at Shine for approximately three, sends part of her salary as monthly remittances to support her young daughter, who resides in Ecuador. Like Lila, Nina is an Ecuadorian Shine employee of three years who has spent five years in the US. She is 28 years old. Table 4.1 provides a summary of this information for each of the four Shine employees whose interview data appear in the analysis presented in this chapter.

Table 4.1 Descriptive data about the four Shine employees whose interview data inform this chapter

Name	Age	Country of Origin	Years in the US	Years at Shine
Dona Aura	55	Portugal	13 years	9 years
Anita	25	Honduras	6 years	4 years
Lila	26	Ecuador	5 years	3 years
Nina	28	Ecuador	5 years	3 years

4.4 Some Linguistic Context: A Brief Comparison of Portuguese vs. Spanish Phonology

As the data for this chapter's analysis are grounded in a Portuguese-Spanish language contact situation, a brief comparison of the phonological features of these two languages aids in an understanding of their specific pairing with respect to Hispanophone and Lusophone employees' ease of communication. As these two languages share a number of syntactic and lexical features, some degree of mutual intelligibility between many varieties allows Spanish and Portuguese speakers to communicate with one another – in limited contexts – through dual-linguality, the simultaneous use of two mutually intelligible languages (Gonçalves, 2013, 2019; Lincoln, 1979; Piller, 2002; Vitale, 2011). As the participants' interviews showed deviation from the standard varieties of their L1s, the information below serves as a rough guide to understanding the linguistic differences that potentially impede mutual intelligibility in spoken contexts.

In terms of spoken language, the property of Spanish as a syllable-timed language vs. Portuguese as a stress-timed language influences vowel lengthening and reduction processes differently in each language: they are far less prominent in Portuguese than in Spanish. For this reason, the vowels of Spanish words are apparent to Lusophones, but the (reduced) vowels that occur in unstressed syllables of Portuguese words may be far less apparent to Hispanophones who have no experience with Portuguese. European – in contrast to Brazilian – Portuguese varieties pose a greater challenge for Spanish speakers' comprehension because of their tendency for more extreme vowel reduction; the resulting syllables, which lack some clearly identifiable vowels, can mislead Spanish speakers to perceive consonant clusters that are not actually present (Ferreira & Holt, 2014).

As the two languages contain numerous cognates, the written versions of the languages are largely comprehensible to readers of both languages with the exception of some differing lexical items. The spoken versions of these languages, however, bring out the phonological differences mentioned above and contribute to unidirectional intelligibility to the untrained ear: Portuguese speakers with limited prior exposure to Spanish can often understand a large percentage of spoken Spanish, which features the vowels that their two written languages share. Spanish speakers with limited prior exposure to Portuguese, however, often struggle to understand much spoken Portuguese. These considerations help to inform the discussion about the Hispanophone employees' strategies to adapt to Shine's Portuguese-centric language policy that follows and, further, the analysis of their ties to the Newark area Portuguese-centric community beyond the Shine community of practice.

4.5 Setting the Scene: Capital, Neoliberalism and the Extended Ironbound Community

The capital associated with the language of powerful groups and entities helps to shape diasporic trajectories (Deumert & Mablanda, 2013). Through individual migrants' increased tendency to 'follow the money' in place of establishing 'close-knit, distinct' ethnically homogenous diaspora communities (Deumert & Mablanda, 2013: 47), a direct link emerges between the shifting nature of diasporic positionality and capital. Moreover, the changes to labor and capital distribution under neoliberalism (Boas & Gans-Morse, 2009) – including the growing prominence of transnational entities and commodification within political, social and economic realms (Heller, 2011; Springer *et al.*, 2016) – indicate a simultaneous shift in capital flows that can directly influence the status of migrant communities. Such dynamics have created settings that diminish traditional attachments to the language(s) of the dominant community (Sabaté i Dalmau, 2013) and counteract the devaluation of migrant languages (conceptualized by Martín Rojo [2013] and Moyer [2018] as *decapitalization*, discussed above).

4.5.1 Cultural capital

As mentioned in the introductory chapter, much of the Ironbound district's semiotic landscape indexes Portuguese culture (Gonçalves, 2012). In addition, Portuguese business owners' common practice of using Portuguese cultural symbols to sell their products creates a marketplace in which the cultural capital of Portuguese often co-exists with its economic capital. Some of these, such as prominent displays of the Portuguese national colors, are apparent to both members of the in-group and out-group; moreover, they bring profits from both of these types of members. In their interviews for this project, customers of Shine who lack ties to the Ironbound or its diaspora community characterize the Ironbound as a place that celebrates its Portuguese identity and is, thus, distinct from the rest of Newark, which they associate with a higher crime rate. The cultural capital that is tied to this Portuguese character comes into focus with these participants' primary reasons for visiting the Ironbound, which include activities such as eating at its Portuguese restaurants and buying Portuguese tiles. For in-group members, more subtle symbols help to tap into nostalgic attachments to the home country. These symbols, together with the use of Portuguese (linguistic capital) to serve customers, heighten the appeal of the given business and contribute to a loyal customer base. Magda, too, has created a business that builds on her own positive stereotypes about Portuguese women (Gonçalves & Schluter, 2017). These stereotypes shape her brand's image which she successfully markets to her clients. In this way, she has commodified (Cameron, 2000; Cavanaugh & Shankar, 2014; Heller, 2011) Shine's Portuguese cultural attachments to create her own niche market. By capitalizing on the promise of superior

Portuguese service while, simultaneously, eliminating 'the liability of foreignness' through marketing and communication that target Anglophone American residents of Westwood, Magda demonstrates the 'contextual intelligence' that emerges from the vantage point of an entrepreneur from a diaspora community (Rana & Elo, 2017: 101), further illustrating her intercultural and emotional competences addressed in Chapter 3.

4.5.2 Social capital

Capital is embedded in networks (Kramsch, 2021; Sommer & Gamper, 2018; Uzzi, 1997; Vigouroux & Mufwene, 2020; Wilson, 1998), and the use of these networks to recruit new employees demonstrates one salient means through which this capital can be identified. With respect to her recruitment method, Magda explains: 'Always they [her cleaning staff] are my source'. Here, she refers to her practice of announcing job vacancies to her employees and tapping into their networks to identify eligible candidates. Although she placed advertisements in newspapers in previous years, she has since made a conscious decision to disseminate news of vacancies at Shine exclusively through word-of-mouth to avoid the time-consuming task of sorting through the hundreds of responses she routinely received to these advertisements. This recruitment practice, thus, highlights the social capital of network membership. The reliance on acquaintances for news of employment opportunities underlines a direct connection between membership in the Newark-area Portuguese-centric network and the heightened prospects of earning a steady income. Employee recruitment through a local migrant network reflects common practice among migrant entrepreneurs (Kloosterman & Rath, 2001), especially those operating within ethnic economies (Pécoud, 2010; Serwe, 2021). This practice underlines the importance of such a positionality for job-seeking migrants relative to their non-migrant counterparts (Gamper, 2015). Within the setting of the current study, the social capital generated and converted through the ability to fit into a predominantly Portuguese-language network helps to demonstrate a way in which capital is intertwined with local and transnational networks (Bourdieu & Wacquant, 1992) that are detached from the dominant culture and the language(s) associated with it.

4.5.3 Economic capital

As the majority of businesses in the Ironbound district of Newark are owned by members of the local Portuguese diaspora and Portuguese is widely spoken within these spaces (Gonçalves, 2012), the economic capital of this community and its ties to Portuguese are on constant display in this section of the city. A business like Magda's that operates an employee service van that runs between the Ironbound, company headquarters, and the houses it cleans is deeply rooted in this Portuguese-centric community. Moreover, Magda's role as the primary language broker between customers and employees, coupled with her lack of confidence in Anglophone workers whom she believes 'don't want to work' (Gonçalves & Schluter, 2017: 249), creates a space in which Lusophone residents' cultural ties and language abilities afford them preferential treatment and can lead to a stable income. This income should not be underestimated given Shine's above industry-average wages and the relatively low turnover rate among Shine employees. With time, many employees manage to afford the purchase of a house and annual holidays in their countries of origin. The example of Shine, thus, represents one of many contexts in the Newark, New Jersey area in which Portuguese-language proficiency has the potential to enhance workers' economic capital.

4.5.4 Transcultural capital and the local Portuguese-centric community in the current era of neoliberalism

The three types of capital outlined above constitute some key origins of power in society (Bourdieu, 1986, 1991). With the shifting nature of capital flows under neoliberalism, new opportunities for more diverse participation in the market have emerged (Duchêne *et al.*, 2013), increasing the potential for migrant businesses to improve their standing within the community (Sabaté i Dalmau, 2013). As transnational networks generate and possess a larger portion of the capital within this context, they also hold more power (cf. Portes *et al.*, 2002) and have given rise to the growing influence of *transcultural capital* (Meinhof & Triandafyllidou, 2006) associated with prominent diaspora groups. Familiarity with the languages associated with these diaspora groups has, thus, increasingly become a source of linguistic capital (DeCosta, 2010).

Lusophone members of the extended Ironbound community are in a position to exploit this transcultural capital most seamlessly: Portuguese-medium communication allows them to make use of their linguistic (cultural) capital, network ties that provide access to jobs represent an important means through which social capital is used, and employment at a Portuguese-centric business helps to build members' economic capital. Those with different ethnolinguistic backgrounds who seek participation in this capital-rich network are, according to the analysis below, able to do so by adapting to its linguistic and cultural orientation. The following analysis draws from interview data to highlight the specific strategies that this orientation inspires among Shine's Hispanophone employees.

4.6 The Mechanics of Fitting in Linguistically: Dual-Linguality or Accommodation to Shine's Portuguese-Centric Orientation?

4.6.1 *Dona Aura's perspective*

Interviews with Magda and her staff show a range of strategies for communication between Hispanophone and Lusophone employees, depending on the overlap of linguistic resources available to the specific pairing of interlocutors. Nevertheless, as reported in Gonçalves and Schluter (2017), many of Shine's Lusophone employees share the opinion that Spanish and Portuguese speakers, despite some of their multilingual repertoires, communicate primarily through *dual-linguality*, described above as the simultaneous use of individuals' different L1s (Gonçalves, 2013, 2019; Lincoln, 1979; Piller, 2002; Vitale, 2011). Because of the differing phonological properties of standard Portuguese and Spanish varieties outlined in the previous section, this strategy is more viable for Lusophones than Hispanophones. Given this potential for one-sided communication challenges, this topic represented one of the foci of the interview questions and sensitized us to potentially divergent Hispanophone and Lusophone perspectives about Shine's internal language(s) of communication.

Dona Aura provides an established Lusophone employee's perspective on achieving mutual intelligibility with her Hispanophone co-workers (Extract (1) below). Each employee differs according to her individual linguistic repertoire; Dona Aura is a noteworthy case because, despite her 13-year residence in the US, she remains largely reliant on Magda to manage her English-language communication with customers and, further, has acquired a very limited Spanish lexicon. The extract begins with her describing the details of communication between Shine's Lusophone and Hispanophone employees.

Extract (1) [interview with Dona Aura, 55, from Portugal]*

1. Dona Aura: *o espanhol entendo bem* (Spanish, I understand well)
2. Anne: *Entende bem?* (You understand well?)
3. Dona Aura: *É, perfeito* (Yes, perfectly)
4. Anne: *Você muda– muda alguma coisa [para melhorar a comunicação?]* (Do you change–
5. change anything [to improve communication)?
6. Dona Aura: *Um **poquito****, é* (A little, yeah)
7. Anne: *Como que você muda?* (How do you change?)
8. Dona Aura: *As vezes a gente fala, erm, elas também entendem o nosso português (.)*
9. (Sometimes we say, erm, they also understand our Portuguese).
10. *elas entendem bem o nosso português e nós entendemos muito bem o espanhol delas*
11. (They understand our Portuguese well, and we understand their Spanish very well.)
12. *é um espanhol muito fácil de aprender* (It's a Spanish that's very easy to learn)
13. Kellie: *Mas por exemplo, você pode dar um exemplo, que você talvez muda...uma palavra?*

14.		(But for example, can you give an example of something that you maybe change…a word?)
15.	Kellie:	*Ou você usa mais o espanhol ou cê sempre fala o português?*
16.		(Or do you use more Spanish or do you always speak in Portuguese?)
17.	Dona Aura:	*Não, eu sempre falo o português* (No, I always speak in Portuguese)
18.	Kellie:	*Então nem uma palavra que fala.* (So not even a word that you say…)
19.	Dona Aura:	*Não porque elas entendam o que eu digo pra elas*
20.		(No because they understand what I say to them)
21.		*e eu entendo o que elas dizem pra mim*
22.		(and I understand what they say to me)
23.	Kellie:	*elas mudam uma coisa* (Do they change anything?)
24.	Dona Aura:	*Sim…Eu não necessito de mudar, porque elas entendem e eu entendo.*
25.		(Yes…I don't need to change because they understand and I understand).

*Original interview in Portuguese
**The Spanish-language diminutive (–ito) appears here instead of its Portuguese equivalent (–inho)

Dona Aura does not regard understanding Spanish as problematic. In fact, she claims to understand Spanish perfectly (line 3). Regarding conversations with her Hispanophone co-workers, she initially claims to modify the way she speaks (line 6), but she later confesses to speaking in Portuguese because her Hispanophone co-workers understand Portuguese and the Lusophone employees understand Spanish (lines 10–11). In line with employees' characterizations of Lusophone-Hispanophone communication practices highlighted in Gonçalves and Schluter (2017), therefore, Dona Aura points to the apparently straightforward practice of dual-linguality to satisfy all employees' communicative needs. As Dona Aura continues, an analysis of her transcript reveals some hints of accommodation. In terms of her accommodation to Spanish-language norms, it is tempting to point to her use of the Spanish-language diminutive *-ito* (instead of its Portuguese equivalent *-inho*) on the word *pouco* (little) (line 6) as evidence; however, a familiarity with the language contact situation of the Ironbound in which some Spanish-language forms have entered the local Portuguese lexicon informs us that use of this form is merely in line with common practice among Lusophones residing in the Newark area.

In terms of Hispanophone employees' accommodation in the direction of Portuguese-language norms, Dona Aura makes some statements that, when looked at more closely, begin to suggest the presence of convergence. With her reference to 'a Spanish that is easy to learn' (line 12), for example, her words suggest a variety of Spanish that has been modified to facilitate Portuguese speakers' understanding. Dona Aura communicates with her co-workers in Portuguese only (line 17) without making any such modifications to enhance its intelligibility. Eventually, she confirms that if a co-worker has to undertake any accommodation work, it is the Spanish speaker who does so (line 24).

Such a nod to Hispanophone employees' accommodation efforts, together with the knowledge of Spanish speakers' potential comprehension challenges in this context, motivated a more comprehensive look into the communicative practices between Hispanophone and Lusophone employees. In our interviews with Shine's four Hispanophone employees, in fact, all of them indicated some degree of convergence to Shine's Portuguese-dominant center. While their comments should be interpreted with the caveat that they do not incorporate a situationally constructed view of communication, they, nevertheless, are worthy of our attention as they provide a picture of Lusophone-Hispanophone communication at Shine that is more complex than the straightforward dual-linguality that comes out of broad mutual intelligibility.

4.6.2 Anita's and Lila's perspectives: The pervasiveness of Portuguese and strategies for accommodation

Anita, Shine's Honduran employee, provides her insights into this topic. In her description of returning home to her Hispanophone husband and mistakenly speaking Portuguese to him after a day at work, she captures the influence of Portuguese on the language practices of Shine's Hispanophone employees. Her example of Portuguese language use (in Extract (2) below) suggests that – contrary to the picture of dual-linguality presented above by Dona Aura – she does not simply speak Spanish to her Lusophone co-workers:

Extract (2) [Interview with Anita, 25, from Honduras]*

1. Anita: ...*As veces estoy hablando en mi casa...y en vez de decir lunes digo* **segunda**.**
(Sometimes when I am speaking at my house and instead of saying *lunes* [Monday in Spanish], I say *segunda* [Monday in Portugese]).
2. *Me confundo porque ya es como paso todo el día con ellas*
(I get confused because it's like I spend the whole day with them)

3. *trato con ellas entonces, ya el hablado ya se me va quedando a mi también.*
(I work together with them so the way of speaking ends up rubbing off on me too).

*Original interview in Spanish
** The Portuguese word for Monday (*segunda*) appears here instead of its Spanish-language equivalent *lunes*

Anita reports using the Portuguese word *segunda* to refer to Monday instead of its Spanish equivalent *lunes* when addressing her Hispanophone husband in the Spanish-language domain of their home (line 1). This example of transfer (line 2) occurs as a result of the extensive time she spends working together with her Lusophone co-workers; furthermore, it suggests, at the very least, a Spanish speaker's active incorporation of Portuguese lexical items to facilitate communication with her Lusophone co-workers. In contrast to Dona Aura's description of the communicative practices between Hispanophone and Lusophone employees, Anita's comments provide an example of a speaker of Shine's minority language whose linguistic efforts to overcome language differences exceed those required for dual-linguality.

Dual-linguality – as put into practice by Dona Aura – envisions the two languages as relatively equal; however, Anita's comments suggest a higher positioning of Portuguese over Spanish during these interactions. This positioning becomes more pronounced with a look at another Hispanophone employee's descriptions of her communication with Lusophone co-workers who, like Dona Aura, have developed minimal skills to communicate with non-Portuguese speakers. Extract (3) comes from an interview with Lila, who borrows lexical items from Portuguese to facilitate effective communication with her Lusophone co-workers:

Extract (3) [Interview with Lila, 26, from Ecuador]*

1. Anne: *Hablas en una manera diferente para dejarlas [las portugesas e brasileñas de*
2. *Shine] entenderte?*
(Do you speak differently in order to allow them [the Portuguese and Brazilian
employees at Shine] to understand you?)
3. Lila: *sí*
(yes)
4. Anne: *Como? Puedes explicar un poco?*
(How? Can you explain a bit?)
5. Lila: *Es como sí por ejemplo a veces ellas no entienden en español hablo en portugués...*

		(It's like for example sometimes they don't understand in Spanish so I speak Portuguese.)
6.	Kellie:	*Então você fala português?**
		(So you speak Portuguese?)
7.	Lila:	*Algunas palabras. Sí.*
		(Some words, yes)
8.	Kellie:	*algunas palabras* **mas não tudo**?
		(Some words but not everything?)
9.	Lila:	**não tudo**
		(Not everything)
10.	Kellie:	**tá bem** (OK)
11.	Lila:	**Mas** *trato, cuando estoy con mi* **namorado** *trato de hablar português,*
12.		*El es-él es português entonces hablamos en casa.*
		(But I try, when I'm with my boyfriend, I try to speak Portuguese,
		he is-he is Portuguese so we speak Portuguese at home.)

*Original in Spanish and Portuguese; words that appear in bold are in Portuguese

In Extract (3) (above), Lila states that she changes the way she speaks when communicating with her Portuguese-speaking co-workers (line 3). If they do not understand her Spanish, she attempts to switch to Portuguese (lines 5) – albeit with a limited Portuguese-language repertoire (line 7) – that she has consciously developed through conversations with her Portuguese boyfriend (lines 11–12). Together, the content of Anita's and Lila's comments show the important role that accommodation (convergence) can play in many of the Hispanophone-Lusophone interactions at Shine.

A closer analysis of Extract (3) provides further insight into the means through which Lila achieves this accommodation. As Kellie is a Portuguese speaker with limited Spanish-language proficiency, Lila's interview transcript provides direct linguistic evidence of her approach to communicating with Portuguese speakers. It features both accurate responses to Portuguese-language interview questions (line 7) and production of some Portuguese by repeating a Portuguese phrase and producing some novel Portuguese words (lines 9 and 11).

In an effort to achieve intelligibility with a Portuguese speaker, Lila chooses Spanish forms that are similar to their Portuguese equivalents, and she borrows words from Portuguese to substitute for words that are dissimilar. For example, *algunas palabras* [some words] (line 7) in Spanish closely resembles *algumas palavras* in Portuguese. In the same way, the Spanish-language phrase from line 11, *quando estoy con mi namorado* [when I am with my boyfriend (Portuguese-language word for boyfriend)]' is very close to its Portuguese translation, *quando estou com meu namorado*. The borrowed Portuguese word in this utterance, *namorado*, is the second part of her communication strategy: she substitutes this word for the Spanish lexical item, *novio*, because it is quite different from its Portuguese equivalent and can potentially lead to misunderstanding. Such a finding allows for a more informed understanding of Anita's comments in Extract (2) about using the Portuguese word, *segunda* (Monday), with her Hispanophone husband. As the Spanish word *lunes* (Monday) differs considerably from its Portuguese equivalent, *segunda*, it could potentially contribute to misunderstandings and communication breakdown if incorporated into conversations with Lusophone co-workers. As Anita needs to actively produce the word to avoid these communication breakdowns, the word, *segunda*, has become particularly salient to her. For these reasons, Anita continues to use it even when she switches to Spanish-dominant domains.

These interpretations from our transcripts are supported by comments made by a second Hispanophone employee from Ecuador, Nina, who specifically mentions in her interview that *cosas que ellas [las hablantes de portugues] no entienden en español nosotros le decimos en portugués* (Things that they [the Portuguese speakers] do not understand in Spanish, we say it in Portuguese). She continues by clarifying that *en el trato son mitad portugués e mitad español palabras* (In practice, they are half Spanish and half Portuguese words). Based on the transcript analysis in the preceding paragraph and Nina's description of her communication with her Portuguese-speaking co-workers here, a clearer picture of a communicative strategy emerges: when needed, Shine's Hispanophone employees can use a hybrid variety that incorporates key Portuguese lexical items while drawing on the Spanish-language phrasings that resemble Portuguese.

This linguistic repertoire suggests an ability to contrastively analyze the two languages, identify potential cross-linguistic challenges and modify utterances to avoid some of them. This strategy reflects Hispanophone employees' cross-language metalinguistic knowledge that distinguishes them from Lusophone co-workers like Dona Aura. This orientation to Portuguese suggests the inherent inequality of the two languages at Shine: while Lusophones like Dona Aura may do little to accommodate to their Hispanophone co-workers, Hispanophone employees, in fact, do not have this option.

Lila's, Nina's and Anita's efforts to accommodate to the linguistic other on the one hand and Dona Aura's lack of accommodation on the other hand shed some light on language and power relations at Shine. As Dona Aura is a core member of the Shine community of practice whose language background aligns with Shine's majority language, she possesses the linguistic capital that allows her to function exclusively in it. Her inability to identify Spanish speakers' efforts to accommodate to her suggests the normativity of European Portuguese (for Dona Aura) by accentuating Hispanophone employees' shortcomings relative to these norms rather than recognizing their distance from Spanish-language norms. This erasure of accommodation strategies from a Lusophone's perspective (like that of Dona Aura) provides a small-scale example of decapitalization (Martín Rojo, 2013; Moyer, 2018) with regard to the devaluation of Spanish. At the same time, it suggests that Portuguese does not undergo this process within Shine-related domains. Moreover, these interlocutors' unequal attempts at convergence parallel findings about accommodation and inequality, which show that speakers of languages with less symbolic power are more likely to undertake the work of accommodation in the direction of speakers of the language with greater symbolic power (Albury & Schluter, 2021; Bourhis, 1991; Stell & Dragojevic, 2017). Asymmetric attempts at convergence, thus, suggest underlying asymmetric power relations, and, through them, Lila's, Nina's and Anita's less powerful positions at Shine.

A Community of Practice perspective (Lave & Wenger; 1991; Wenger, 1998) fits the above analysis insofar as the Hispanophone employees look to established, core figures at Shine – all of whom are Lusophone given the company's founding principles and original employees – to learn the norms of communicative practices within the company that allow them to index ingroup membership. Moreover, the blue-collar context of the workplace, with its common practice of apprenticing, helps to bring to mind this mentor-mentee relationship. Lila's and Anita's comprehension of Portuguese and modification of potentially incomprehensible Spanish words demonstrate adaptation to Shine's shared Portuguese-dominant repertoires. Power structures within communities of practice tend to reproduce those that exist within their larger-scale settings (Contu & Willmott, 2003; Kramsch, 2021; Pietikäinen & Kelly-Holmes, 2013). This is also the case for the convergence practices at Shine, which are largely in line with those of the extended Ironbound community. The following section addresses this scale by zooming out to the larger community. At the same time, it also shifts the primary focus of analysis from capital ownership – together with its relationship to power dynamics – to the other two aspects of investment: identity and ideology. Subsequent to this discussion, it becomes possible to outline the interplay between these three constructs vis-à-vis Hispanophone employees' orientations to the Portuguese-centric community.

4.7 Analyzing Orientations to Portuguese-Centricity Beyond the Shine Community of Practice: A Focus on Ideology and Identity

The previous section highlighted the language practices and power dynamics that reflect Lila's and Anita's positionalities with respect to Shine's Lusophone speakers. As positionality is grounded in larger-scale ideologies that inform constructions of identity (Darvin & Norton,

2015), this section now turns to the ideologies that come out of Shine's embeddedness within the extended Ironbound community. The extent to which membership in a new migrant community suits these ideologies represents the second topic addressed here: articulations of identity.

Extract (4) comes from Nina, one of Shine's Ecuadorian employees. In it, her ideologies about other Ecuadorian immigrants emerges. She distinguishes this group from her Lusophone co-workers and friends, whom she views more favorably. Analysis of this extract helps to contextualize Nina's decision to work at Shine instead of one of the many Hispanophone Latino-managed cleaning companies in the area. In this way, it is possible to trace Nina's comments to ideologies beyond the Shine community of practice:

Extract (4) [Interview with Nina, 28, from Ecuador]*

1. Nina: *Tengo muchos amigos ecuatorianos, pero es como qué si tú tienes más ellos*
2. *quieren tener y es como que te miran de lado…*
(I have a lot of Ecuadoran friends but it's it's like if you have more they want to
have it and it's like they are sizing you up…)
3. *me gusta el trato de los portugueses e de los brasileiros. Tengo amistades brasileiras*
4. *que frecuento mucho.*
(I like the way the Portuguese and the Brazilians treat people. I have Brazilian
friends who I see a lot).
5. *es… soy así prefiero mi vida mi mundo aparte de la gente que me conoce.*
(It's…I am like that I prefer my life my world apart from the people who know me).

*Original in Spanish

In Extract (4), Nina describes her fellow Ecuadorians as jealous (lines 1–2) and insincere. She contrasts her negative evaluation of Ecuadorians with her Portuguese and Brazilian acquaintances, whose approach to relationships she characterizes in positive terms (line 3). While Nina has a lot of Ecuadorian friends (line 1), she chooses to spend her free time primarily with her Lusophone friends (lines 3–4). In fact, she consciously distances herself from her own migrant community and expresses a desire to build a separate life from them (line 5).

Nina's comments help to expose her negative ideologies toward Ecuadorians and positive ideologies toward Lusophones, which, together, inform her separation from the local Ecuadorian diaspora and integration into the extended Ironbound community. Moreover, these ideologies directly reflect those of Lila, who, in her interview, juxtaposes the 'self-centered' and unhelpful character of Hispanophone Latinos with her 'more sociable' and helpful Portuguese acquaintances (see Chapter 3, Extract 12 for the complete extract). In fact, similar connections also emerged during analysis of the data from the other two Hispanophone employees, and these findings highlight the four Hispanophone employees' shared orientation to the Ironbound's Portuguese-centric community beyond the domains of Shine. Demographic data collected during our fieldwork, for example, point to all four of these employees' residences in Portuguese-dominant districts in either Newark or Elizabeth, New Jersey; moreover, each of them describes their neighborhoods as preferable alternatives to residence in Spanish or English-dominant districts. The development of strategies that contribute to successful daily communication within these Portuguese-dominant districts is integral to these residential choices.

Analysis of these ideologies acknowledges their rootedness in the power structures that inform hegemonic forces (DeCosta, 2010). While the negative ideologies toward Ecuadorians and other Hispanophone Latinos highlighted above quite possibly reflect discrimination of these groups within larger power structures, the data collected for this project are inadequate for addressing this issue. Of primary focus here, instead, are the positive ideologies toward the extended Ironbound community and the social structures from which they stem. Embedded within these structures, these participants' positive ideologies guide them to construct professional and social lives that strengthen their Lusophone network ties while weakening those with members of their own diaspora communities. In this way, the data presented here provide evidence of an alternative diaspora group that generates positive ideologies that have typically been reserved for the dominant culture.

Ideologies such as these are considered a defining feature of ethnolinguistic identity construction (Darvin & Norton, 2015: 43), the topic to which the current discussion now turns. For the purposes of providing a more detailed example of this process, the case of Nina receives primary focus here.

Further data from Nina's interview transcript, together with comments from Magda's interview and our own observations, suggest that Portuguese and the local Portuguese-centric culture feature prominently in Nina's social life. In addition to developing her Portuguese-language competence through her interactions with her Brazilian friends, her relationship with Magda – which stretches into non-work-related domains and includes social visits to Magda's sister's house – also provides ample opportunities. Under the tutelage of Magda and her sister, too, she has recently mastered a regional Brazilian culinary staple from Minas Gerais (Magda's home state) that has become a favorite of the extended

Ironbound community, cheese bread (*pão de queijo*), which she now prepares regularly for her own family. Participation in such activities highlights Nina's affective attachment (Chatterjee & Schluter, 2020) to her Lusophone network that transcends professional boundaries, resulting in her 'thank[ing] God for bringing Magda into her life'. In these ways, Nina's language and cultural acquisition efforts allow for 'the construction of the identities [she] desire[s] and the communities [she] wants to join in order to engage in communication and social life' (Canagarajah, 2004: 117).

In line with her positive ideologies toward the local Portuguese-centric diaspora community, her active Brazilian social network, and her attempts at acquiring cultural knowledge, Nina's employment at Shine reflects a larger effort to become a member of a community that she views more favorably than her own. Nina adopts qualities that allow her to move closer to her *imagined identity* (Norton, 2000, 2013) as a member of a community of people who, in contrast to her descriptions of fellow Ecuadorians, she believes approach each other with sincerity. In Darvin and Norton's (2015: 46) words, 'Whether it is because learners want to be part of a country or a peer group, to seek romance, or to achieve financial security, learners invest because there is something they want for themselves'. In this case, the greater *financial stability* that comes out of Nina's close relationship with her employer and the enhanced access to desirable *peer groups*, like that of her Brazilian friends and Magda's family, represent the benefits that come with her investment in Portuguese language and culture. Nina, thus, invests (Darvin & Norton, 2015; Norton, 2000) in these aspects to enhance her in-group status among members of this group. Although this investment does not extend to Nina's choice of romantic partner, Lila's comments from Extract (3) provide an example in which investment in Portuguese language and culture also fulfills the romantic aspirations described above. Employment at Shine, with its Portuguese-centric orientation, thus, represents only one part of a more general positionality that ties together participants' identities and ideologies. The perceived benefits of this positionality, as the following section highlights, are rooted in the growing prominence of the Portuguese-centric diaspora within the local community that comes out of increased ownership of capital (Darvin & Norton, 2015). As a result, this diaspora can function as a viable alternative to the dominant Anglophone culture for those who, like the participants highlighted here, have the linguistic and cultural knowledge to access it.

4.8 Putting It All Together: Capital, Identity, Ideology, Agency and Diasporic Belonging

In this section, we briefly bring together the various factors that contribute to our discussion of employment at Shine and the choices that drive these decisions among Hispanophone Latina workers. As we discussed above, individuals' abilities to shift orientations further parallel the dynamic nature of ideologies and identity construction (Darvin, 2016), both of which can adjust to suit the changing shape of power asymmetries that are largely driven by capital. The distinction between this vision of dynamism and that which is informed by the relatively static concept of reproduction (Bourdieu, 1977) highlights individuals' heightened agentive capacity. By carrying out the choice to orient to an alternative diaspora group, the participants profiled in this chapter provide an example of the interplay between individual action and sociocultural structures (via ideologies) that characterize agency (Ahearn, 2001; Block, 2012). Specifically, they provide evidence to support conceptions of agency that recognize structure's influential – albeit not hegemonic – relationship to individuals' capacity to act (Archer, 2000, 2007; Ortner, 2006), especially in terms of orientations to foreign languages (Miller, 2016).

4.9 Chapter Summary

Despite the two languages' phonological characteristics that contribute to higher levels of Spanish-language intelligibility among Lusophones (relative to Portuguese-language intelligibility among Hispanophones), convergence efforts take place primarily in the direction of Portuguese and are largely invisible to the dominant group. Following Bourhis (1991) and Stell and Dragojevic (2017), these findings point to underlying inequalities. As communities of practice tend to reproduce the power asymmetries of their settings (Contu & Willmott, 2003; Pietikäinen & Kelly-Holmes, 2013), the positionality that informs this practice within Shine extends – through residential and social network choices – into non-employment domains within the Newark-based, Portuguese-centric diaspora community in which Shine is embedded. In line with Darvin and Norton (2015), this positionality lies at the intersection between positive ideologies toward the local Portuguese-centric diaspora community and participants' resulting construction of identities as members of this community; moreover, the benefits of affiliating with these identities are rooted in this group's ownership of capital. The analysis presented here points to Hispanophone employees' agentive re-conceptualization of their identities as members of the Newark-area, Portuguese-centric diaspora community, providing a novel example of horizontal assimilation (Prashad, 2001). Their resulting positionality is, therefore, not limited to the two options of alignment with the local, dominant culture vs. that of the homeland. Instead, the findings highlight the additional option – made possible through the increased dispersion of capital in the current era (Duchêne *et al.*, 2013) – of orienting to an ethnolinguistically different diaspora group that has power within the local community. Moreover, these findings provide a US-based, blue-collar contribution to work on language at the workplace and beyond: while multilingual employees of white-collar businesses may display a tendency to converge toward English as a lingua franca (Angouri, 2014; Jonsson & Blåsjo, 2020; Kleifgen, 2013; Lønsmann & Mortensen, 2018), the results from the preceding analysis, in line with (Goldstein, 1997), suggest the sustained prestige of core members' L1 in blue-collar work contexts. The work presented in this chapter extends these findings to the ethnic enclaves inhabited by these core members, drawing attention to the need to re-evaluate the influence of decapitalization within these types of settings.

5 Multicompetence as Essential and English-Language Proficiency as Secondary: Examining the Shape of Customer–Employee Interactions between Speakers who do not Share a Common Language

5.1 Introduction

Set in the households that Shine serves, this chapter provides a space in which to address the primary question that initially inspired this project: How does communication actually work between English-speaking customers and their domestic workers who rate their English-language abilities as poor? Responses to this inquiry have led to the larger examination of the communicative role of objects, gestures, human touch and technology that help to support and, in some cases, substitute for linguistic resources in customer–employee interactions. In doing so, it highlights examples of multicompetent resourcefulness between interlocutors who do not share a lingua franca. The concepts of *multicompetence* (Cook, 1991, 2016), *embodied sociolinguistics* (Bucholtz & Hall, 2016), *translanguaging* to include multimodality (Li, 2018), *nexus analysis* (Scollon & Scollon, 2004), *transidioma* (Jacquemet, 2016) and *Post-Humanist Applied Linguistics* (Pennycook, 2018) provide the principal contributions to the theoretical grounds for this analysis. The resulting discussion assesses the importance of English in this context.

The privileged position of Portuguese – both at Shine and within the extended Ironbound community – has been a central focus of this book thus far. As detailed in Chapter 3, a complementary emphasis includes Magda's role as Shine's primary language broker: her ability to convey customers' English-language requests to her Lusophone and Hispanophone employees allows Shine-external communication to function smoothly. Absent from this picture are the numerous daily customer–employee interactions that result in successful meaning negotiation despite the lack of a shared language. For this reason, the extra-linguistic processes that allow for such communication represent the primary subject of analysis in this chapter. While English-language proficiency has emerged as a key component of Magda's communication success, the analysis presented throughout this chapter highlights its secondary role in employees' direct interactions with customers. In this context, speakers' effective deployment of communicative resources that draw on their multicompetence represents a more important ability. This focus allows us to seek out answers to the following guiding questions: What are the extra-linguistic means through which English-dominant customers and Shine employees successfully communicate with one another? What do these findings suggest about the importance of English in these encounters?

As mentioned in Chapter 1, language is a widely discussed means through which interlocutors express and perceive meaning; however, it represents only one of a variety of communicative resources that are deployed in conjunction with one another (Birdwhistell, 1970; Canagarajah, 2013; García & Li, 2014; Gonçalves, 2020a; Goodwin, 2000; Kusters, 2021; Kusters *et al.*, 2017; Lindström *et al.*, 2017; McElhinny, 2015). Indeed, this perspective aligns with Blommaert's as quoted in (Sherris & Adami, 2019: 24–25) vision of language as the following:

> One of many resources that are deployed in social interaction. And of all these resources, it is the most overrated. It is overrated because popular beliefs equate 'communication' and 'language', and so attribute way too much weight to the role of language (as 'correct' mapping of form over denotational content) in meaning-making…People have to share a mutually ratified set of communicative resources, and if no such resources are readily available, they will construct them ad hoc.

This vision of language as one of the various tools of communication represents a central component of our analysis, which presents examples that demonstrate interlocutors' communicative/semiotic repertoires rather than merely focusing on linguistic aspects (Canagarajah, 2020, 2021; Gonçalves, 2020a; Hymes, 1969; Kusters, 2021; Kusters *et al.*, 2017; Rymes, 2014). With this approach, it follows Blommaert (in Sherris & Adami, 2019: 25) through its focus on the 'set of communicative resources' that Shine employees and customers have either 'mutually ratified' or 'constructed ad hoc'. In line with Coupland's (2016) call to reconsider how sociolinguistic change is theorized by venturing beyond language and account for societal changes taking place, this chapter addresses different types of modalities and meta-communication employed by interlocutors to achieve communicative aims. As such, this chapter focuses on the de-centering of language. With this de-centering of language, the following discussion simultaneously de-privileges the role of English-language proficiency.

While sociolinguistic scholarship through the years has, at times, emphasized multimodal aspects of communication (cf. Blommaert, 2010; Thurlow & Jaworski, 2014; also see chapters in Coupland, 2016; Sherris & Adami, 2019, and others), recent work in the field has more systematically acknowledged linguistic tools as only one part of the broader picture of communication. In doing so, this work has expanded the range of extra-linguistic resources that receive research attention. Embodied sociolinguistics (Bucholtz & Hall, 2016), for example, draws attention to the important role of the body in communication. The Post-Humanist perspective (Pennycook, 2018), for its part, emphasizes the creative, diverse resources that individuals agentively deploy to interact with one another. Given the central role of embodied interaction and the relatively peripheral role of language in certain multilingual contexts, in fact, some of the literature replaces the notion of 'linguistic repertoires' with 'semiotic repertoires' to place equal importance on the ways in which individuals' bodies participate in meaning transmission (Gonçalves, 2020a; Kusters, 2021; Kusters *et al.*, 2017). Updates to the theory of *translanguaging* also incorporate these themes to refer to the entirety of all communicative resources as a single unified system (Li, 2018).

First conceptualized by Vivian Cook in 1991, the concept of multicompetence was formulated as a theory of second language acquisition to contest deficit models that measure an L2 speaker's proficiency with respect to that of native speakers. The exact definition of multicompetence has developed through the years to follow emerging trends, with the most recent iteration referring to 'the overall system of a mind or a community that uses more than one language' (Cook, 2016: 3). In addition to maintaining its independence from the norms set by monolingual native speakers, this understanding of multicompetence aligns with notions of translanguaging (Li, 2018) through its unified vision of communicative resources from different languages as one total cognitive system. Moreover, this concept moves beyond linguistic resources with its reference to the 'system of a mind or community' that is built on the premise that 'multi-competence affects the whole mind, i.e. all language and cognitive systems, rather than language alone' (Cook, 2016: 15). Indeed, the flexible, resourceful interlocutors discussed in this chapter demonstrate different linguistic and non-linguistic means through which multicompetence can be realized in the absence of a lingua franca. While some features of multicompetence discussed below – including comfort with ambiguity and behavioral flexibility – overlap with some of the tenets of intercultural competence (Chan, 2023), a comprehensive discussion of intercultural competence is beyond the scope of this chapter.

5.2 Linguistic and Extra-Linguistic Resources within the Multilingual Workplace

Blackledge and Creese (2017) bring both the concepts of translanguaging and semiotic repertoires into the multilingual workplace as a means of analyzing the transfer of meaning between workers and customers who share a space but do not share a language. As the minimal overlap between interlocutors' linguistic resources also features prominently in Shine's customer–employee interactions, we draw on this work's emphasis on multimodal and semiotic resources to address the forms through which successful communication takes place within the Shine workplace domain.

This approach departs from the literature that has foregrounded the role of language in the globalized neoliberal economy (Heller, 2003). While work that addresses the commodification of communication skills in the current neoliberal era (Urciuoli, 2008) potentially broadens the discussion to include extra-linguistic resources, much of the literature (including some of our own previous work) focuses explicitly on linguistic aspects of communication (cf. Duchêne, 2009; Duchêne *et al.*, 2013). In it, instrumentality tends to be tied to proficiency in either the dominant language or a lingua franca. This is certainly the case, for example, in Lorente's (2012, 2017) descriptions of Filipina 'supermaids' whose nimble English-speaking tongues are marketed to suggest an ease of communication with potential employers and, as such, a key component of a productive, harmonious working relationship. The following analysis of participants' communication strategies also addresses the importance of English-language proficiency for fulfilling Shine-related work duties. By fulfilling these duties, employees maintain their good standing at Shine, allowing some of them to rise in the company hierarchy over time to become upwardly mobile.

5.3 Lusophone Perspectives for Analysis: The Cases of Marcela, Maria Clara and Adriana

While preceding chapters have largely focused on interview and observation data collected from Shine's owner and her Hispanophone employees, the data presented in this chapter complement this perspective by foregrounding the interview data of three of Shine's Lusophone employees: Marcela, Maria Clara and Adriana, which we will describe in more detail in the coming discussion.

Marcela (38 years old): at the time of our interview, Marcela had been residing in the US for six years and working for Shine for nearly two. She comes from Brazil, where her two children (aged 16 and 13) continue to reside. In Brazil, she worked primarily as a bartender, and, subsequent to her employment at a restaurant in Newark, began working at Shine. In the US, she remarried a European Portuguese man and took a beginner's English course for three months. According to the information she provided in her interview, she understands European Portuguese and Spanish; furthermore, she tries to use Spanish with Hispanophone co-workers and, even, a select number of customers who possess some proficiency in the language. Although she is motivated to improve her English, she describes her current level as 'very basic'.

Maria Clara: Shine's oldest employee at age 63, Maria Clara is a retired, university-educated teacher from Brazil. At the time of our interview, she had lived in the Portuguese-dominant Ironbound District of Newark for 10 years and had acquired a very limited repertoire of English. She is also undocumented. Residing in the Ironbound neighborhood, she interacts primarily with Lusophone and Hispanophone friends. English plays a very minor role in her daily communication. She originally moved to the US to be with her only son and his family. Although her son had recently been deported to Brazil, Maria Clara stayed in the US in order to remain close to her four-year-old grandchild, who resides with her mother and is the subject of her son's custody battle. At work, she uses very little English with clients and admits to relying on body language and gestures in order to communicate with them.

Adriana (40 years old): is a Portuguese employee who has lived in the US for 23 years and worked at Shine for 22. Despite her long residence in the US, Adriana considers her English to be rudimentary. She has never attended English-language classes nor developed any interest in acquiring more English-language resources, which she deems to be of very limited relevance to her daily life. On the occasions in which English is helpful, she relies on her daughter, Julia (discussed in Chapter 3) to serve as a language broker in various contexts. At Shine, Adriana performs two important functions in addition to her duties as a driver and cleaner. These include collaboration with Magda on the weekly schedule and visits to new clients' houses to familiarize the company and customers with one another. According to Magda and her customers, Adriana is a loyal and diligent worker who has a lot of energy and a very optimistic attitude. She infuses both of these traits into her interviews. Magda describes Adriana as her best employee; her positive personal and professional traits have allowed her to climb Shine's hierarchy to the number two position of assistant manager.

Together, Marcela's, Maria Clara's and Adriana's ethnographic data contribute to a picture of multimodality in employee–customer interactions. They provide a range of strategies that include the use of material objects, gestures, collaboration with the customers and computer-assisted multimodality. Moreover, their perspectives are grounded in different viewpoints regarding the necessity of language for the highlighted interactions. In this way, they reveal a contrast between a language-centered vs. language de-centered approach to multilingual communication. This diversity of strategies and orientations helps to enhance the overall representativeness of the findings that emerge.

5.4 The Use of Artifacts, Gestures and Language to Convey Meaning

5.4.1 Employees' use of their bodies and artifacts in a community of practice

Marcela succeeds in communicating directly with Shine customers despite her limited English-language resources. She accomplishes this through a pre-established sequence of multimodal strategies, which she discusses briefly in Extract (1) below.

Extract (1) [interview with Marcela, 38, from Brazil]*

1. Marcela: *Eu falo uma coisa e elas não, óbvio...não tão entendendo o que eu tô dizendo.*
2. *Às vezes eu tenho que fazer a mesma um, um gesto alguma coisa mais prático.*
(I say something and they obviously...aren't understanding what I'm saying. Sometimes I have to make a gesture. Something more practical.)
3. *Por exemplo eu preciso de mais produto então eu deixo, faço assim lá põe em*
4. *cima do guardanapo se não tem ninguém em casa.*
(For example I need more of a given product, so I leave it. I put it there on a
napkin if there is no one at the house).
5. *Se tem [alguém em casa], já falo pra ela o que eu preciso e já ponho no lixo.*
(If there is [someone at home] I just say to her what I need and I put it in the
garbage can).

*Original interview in Portuguese

Extract (1) above describes a multimodal approach to requesting the purchase of cleaning products that have been used up during house cleaning activities. Marcela first tries to request the product through linguistic means; however, the use of this resource is ineffective (line 1). For this reason, she shifts to a non-linguistic strategy, which she refers to as a 'gesture' that is 'more practical' (line 2). The choice of strategy changes depending on the customer's presence: if the customer is absent, Marcela places the empty container on a napkin (line 4); if the customer is present, she simply states the name of the product as she throws the empty container into the garbage can (line 5).

In this example, the utterance of the product's name represents the only feature of the successful interaction that is strictly linguistic; embodied communication and manipulation of objects in space, instead, convey much of Marcela's intended meaning. Considered a form of 'intersubjectivity', the coordinated use of artifacts and embodied interaction has been well documented within the fields of Conversation Analysis and Interactional Sociolinguistics (Canagarajah, 2020; Mondada, 2022; Streeck *et al.*, 2011). While this strand also includes studies that analyze service encounters (cf. Lindström *et al.*, 2017, for a thorough review), it has largely neglected contexts in which interlocutors share minimal linguistic resources, as is the case here. Marcela's emphasis on embodied materiality provides new insights when viewed through the lenses of multimodality and multicompetence. As this strategy sufficiently serves Marcela's communicative needs, it simultaneously renders proficiency in the dominant language less relevant.

Through our ethnographic observations and document analysis (see Chapter 2 for a thorough discussion of these methods), we learned that the technique of placing a product on a napkin to request its purchase was developed by Magda and introduced to customers and employees during orientation periods. Moreover, it is also included in the seven-page manual that every new customer receives as part of Magda's initial household consultation. Such an emphasis on this communicative action underlines the relevance of *nexus analysis* (Scollon & Scollon, 2004), which considers actions (rather than language and culture) as the primary focus of analysis in ethnographies of communication. Communicative resources are, according to this lens, deployed as a part of a *nexus of practice* – understood as a 'semiotic ecosystem' – in which 'historical trajectories of people, places, discourse, ideas, and objects come together' (Scollon & Scollon, 2004: 159). The 'people' in this context include Shine employees and customers, and these multimodal practices hold currency specifically within the 'places' in which they meet: the households that Shine serves.

Similarly to the multimodal communicative conventions developed within a multilingual high-tech company (Kleifgen, 2013), this example reflects the heightened ability to convey meaning through semiotic means that have already been established between members of the same community of practice (Lave & Wenger, 1991; Wenger, 1998). Membership within this community of practice, thus, represents a key to understanding this specific multimodal message. Moreover, as discussed further in the next section, the ability to express oneself successfully in this context places importance on both the individual who initiates the communicative act as well as her interlocutor who deduces its meaning.

5.4.2 Shine's customers as collaborators in multimodal meaning-making

Marcela's comments provide insight into a semiotic speech act initiated by a Shine employee. While its expression relies on her actions, it is also important to recognize the role of the customer for its accurate interpretation. Extract (2) (below) extends this theme to include a discussion of customers who use diverse strategies to either act as collaborators or the primary performers of this work. In it, Maria Clara describes the nature of her communication with customers.

Extract (2) [Interview with Maria Clara, 63, from Brazil]*

1. Maria Clara: *Me pedem alguma coisa f-alam inglês. Eu peço pra falar bem devagar, repetir...*
(They ask me something in English. I ask them to speak very slowly and to repeat...)
2. *Ou através de mímica. Os americanos usam muito mímica, sabem que a gente*
3. *não fala bem o inglês.*
(Or through gestures. Americans use a lot of gestures. They know that we don't speak English well...)
4. *Em tudo que eles pedem eles já quase que, fazem a mímica pra você*
5. *entender... 'Fecha a porta' [gestures] 'lock the door'**
(For everything they ask, they almost always use gestures to get you to understand. 'Close the door' [gestures] 'Lock the door')

*Original interview in Portuguese
**This phrase occurs in English

Maria Clara enlists customers' help by asking them to modify their speech (line 1). Furthermore, based on her experience with her customers, she concludes that Americans 'almost always' (line 4) perform much of the accommodation work through their frequent use of accompanying gestures (line 2) to overcome non-overlapping linguistic resources. Maria Clara provides an example by pairing the gesture of locking the door together with an imitation of customers' uttering the English words, 'lock the door' in a slowly enunciated manner (line 5). Consisting of an imperative verb and an object, it is noteworthy that customers use a simple sentence structure to convey the linguistic aspects of their message, which is already reinforced through the aforementioned gesture. In this way, Maria Clara points to customers' collaboration through both linguistic and extra-linguistic means.

In addition to providing more data that emphasize the relevance of embodied communicative practice, Extract (2) also helps to highlight the concomitant use of the body and language in support of one another. In this way, they serve as an example to show the inextricable nature of embodied and linguistic resources, which function as components of an individual's single, unified communicative repertoire (Li, 2018). Similar to the embodied strategies employed by customers and employees who share minimal language-specific resources in marketplace and shop contexts (Blackledge & Creese, 2017; Hua *et al.*, 2017), this example highlights an instance in which the comprehension of gestures represents an essential component of overall comprehension in a particular language contact zone.

Although the local register used for general working encounters in Westwood (the town of Shine's headquarters) reflects this district's high level of education through its widespread incorporation of standard American English features, Shine's Anglophone customers orient, together with Maria Clara and Marcela, to the situation-specific scale by complementing their language with gestures to convey meaning. This finding reflects Blommaert's reminder of the important role played by 'uptake' for carrying out successful communication: he views 'the need for others [to enable] us to be communicating beings' as 'the most crucial constraint' that determines the strategies that interlocutors deploy (Blommaert, as cited in Sherris & Adami, 2019: 24). While Shine employees' speech features various English-language lexical borrowings and demonstrate a way in which the locally dominant language influences that of the migrant population, the American customers' modification of their communicative strategies to suit their Lusophone interlocutors suggests that the opposite is also true: consistent with the findings from Tarrow (2005) and Blommaert *et al.* (2005), these examples highlight the ways in which language contact situations also influence the autochthonous population's approach to communication.

In the extracts highlighted above, Marcela provides an example of employees' manipulation of objects in space to communicate meaning specific to the household cleaning domain. Maria Clara's description of customers' use of gestures provides an example of embodied communication that suggests that, similar to the employees, they, too, draw on extra-linguistic resources from their semiotic repertoires to facilitate communication in this space. In both of these cases, multimodal strategies are deployed to compensate for the absence of a lingua franca between customers and employees. Despite the emphasis on multimodality in the analysis, therefore, the extracts presented above suggest that Marcela and Maria Clara implicitly envision linguistic resources as primary and extra-linguistic resources as secondary. This perception demonstrates the common habit of 'foregrounding speech' over other modalities (Loncke *et al.*, 2006: 170; see also Kusters, 2021; Kusters *et al.*, 2017) even though past and current research points out the importance of non-linguistic communicative resources.

The data from Adriana that appear below switch these points of emphasis. As her interview extract shows, she does not consider language proficiency as fundamental to establishing an understanding with customers, especially in light of easy access to digital technologies. With this de-emphasis on language, Adriana's perspective also points to a diminished importance of overlaps between employees' and customers' English-language repertoires.

5.5 Multicompetence, Digital Technologies and Diminished Investment

Unlike her co-workers, Adriana expresses comfortable acceptance of apparent gaps in her understanding of English. This comfort arises in part through her successful deployment of embodied, multisensory communication. In the situations that rely on deeper linguistic knowledge, she employs a strategy that allows her to do so without acquiring any additional language: she turns to digital translations.

Extract (3) [Interview with Adriana, 40 years old, from Portugal]*

1. *Eu acho que não preciso muito saber alguma coisa que eu às vezes*
    (I think it's not really necessary to know something that I sometimes)
2. *não entenda. Agora hoje em dia todas as traduções a gente já tem no aparelho, tem*
    (don't understand. Now these days all of the translations we have on a device,)
3. *no telephone, tem no pequenino, no computador pequeno. A gente vai e traduz*
    (we have on the phone, on the tiny thing, on the small computer. We go and translate)
4. *uma palavra ou outra que não sabe desenrasca-se.*
    (one word or another that we can't figure out.)

*Interview originally in Portuguese

In Extract (3) (above), Adriana explains that she does not strive to acquire the components of language that would allow for full linguistic comprehension (lines 1–2). Moreover, the need for acquiring a larger English-language vocabulary has become less important in the age of translation software and mobile applications that supply/translate unknown words (lines 3–4). Such tools, Adriana argues, diminish the need for language learning, especially because these technologies are easy to use and widely available on phones and computers.

Adriana's use of digital translations enables her to fuse on-line communication with her off-line, face-to-face interactions with customers. This seamless integration of technology as part of a larger communicative repertoire has received considerable attention in the literature with respect to the contextual properties of multimodality in which communication is embedded (Androutsopoulos, 2006, 2021; Kress, 2009; Scollon & Levine, 2004). Following its inclusion in Li Wei's updated (2018) work 'Translanguaging as a Practical Theory of Language' and Pennycook's (2018) *Post-Humanist* perspective, this union between digital and more traditional forms of expression now represents a widespread focus of analysis. Through its investigation into altered power relations that stem from this phenomenon, the concept of *transidioma* (Jacquemet, 2005, 2016) is particularly relevant to this discussion. For, in Adriana's case, her access to digital translations serves as an agentive means through which to deflect the shame – felt by some of her co-workers – for a low level of communicative competence in the dominant language. In this way, it represents an important resource that boosts her confidence that she can grasp important ideas without needing to understand each micro-level component of a given text, thereby positioning her as a multicompetent (Cook, 1991, 2016) rather than limited English-proficient speaker.

This heightened degree of agency also influences Adriana's perception of the relative prestige of English-language communicative competence. Ideologies that emphasize the need to acquire the dominant language for success in the US regularly contribute to deficit perspectives (Valencia, 2010), invoking shame among some workers who cannot use English as their primary mode of communication with Anglophone customers. Adriana's interview comments, which carry importance because they come from a highly successful communicator, present a contrasting view: she attaches little prestige to English-language communicative competence and expresses no shame for this stance.

Adriana's comments link increased access to translations with a diminished need to *invest* (Norton, 2000) in a foreign language, and, in this way, reflect the need to revisit notions of investment to remain relevant to 21st-century practices (Darvin & Norton, 2015). As the use of these devices reduces reliance on language brokering by Shine's owner, they are consistent with Darvin and Norton (2015) who associate them with greater autonomy. Moreover, employees' enhanced ability to discuss cleaning issues that arise directly with the customers in real time and to take action to resolve these issues provides an example of the heightened degree of agency available to language learners in the current digital era (Darvin & Norton, 2015). Such autonomy and agency reflect the increased symbolic capital that comes with access to this technology. This symbolic capital can be converted into economic capital in the case of employees who, independently of Shine, arrange additional cleaning jobs directly with homeowners or, in the case of Adriana, rise in Shine's hierarchy to a position that requires more intense and potentially complex communication with customers. When considering Adriana's wider perspective, in fact, this use of technology to avoid investing more deeply in language acquisition directly aligns with her emphasis on multisensorial – rather than strictly linguistic – forms of communication. While work that addresses investment in the digital era has tended to investigate foreign-language investment through digital technologies (cf. Lexander & Androutsopoulos, 2021, 2023; Sultana & Dovchin, 2020; Thapa, 2019), the findings presented here suggest that these technologies themselves may also contribute to reduced investment in a given foreign language, especially in the case of a learner who has already developed a rich extra-linguistic repertoire. Although such generative AI services as Chat GPT were not yet available during the time of data collection, it is highly likely that access to such tools has strengthened this effect.

5.6 Reflections on Multimodality with Respect to the Preceding Analyses

The above analysis addresses the ways through which extra-linguistic resources influence customer-employee communication in the Shine household cleaning space. Marcela's interview extract highlights an example of multimodal, semiotic communication through the customers' and employees' shared orientation to pre-established conventions within the Shine community of practice, allowing them to coordinate their interpretations of specific embodied and material modalities. Marcela shows flexibility by adapting her strategy depending on the customer's ability to understand her English and the presence/absence of the customer. In this case, she does not rely on the spontaneous, creative deployment of resources, but, rather, the tapping into the existing nexus of practice (Scollon & Scollon, 2004) with which all experienced interlocutors in the interactional space are familiar.

Customers' and employees' co-construction of meaning within the nexus of practice, as highlighted in Marcela's interview extract, helps to draw attention to customers' roles in customer–employee interactions, which Maria Clara's interview extract emphasizes. Through their coordination of embodied and linguistic strategies with Shine employees, customers adapt their communicative approach to draw on the resources they share with employees. In this way, they adjust their orientation so that it aligns with that of their interlocutors. Blommaert (in Sherris & Adami, 2019) reminds us that 'uptake' represents a central component of effective communication. Customers' recognition of the need to be understood by employees ultimately helps to determine the success of the space-specific communicative practices that emerge.

Adriana envisions language as only one aspect of space-specific communicative practices. Her rise to the top of Shine has resulted, in large part, from her establishment and maintenance of strong relationships with customers. A flawless linguistic understanding of customers' utterances does not provide the foundation for these relationships. Her recognition of this non-linguistic foundation contributes to her multi-competent (Cook, 2016) perspective, which places importance on the communicative resources that she has demonstrated rather than any perceived shortcomings in her English-language proficiency. Moreover, her ability to draw on digital translations as needed reinforces this perspective.

A primary aim of the preceding analysis includes exploring the role of English in the interactional space shared by Shine's customers and employees. Before fully addressing this topic, a disclaimer is in order. English carries considerable symbolic value on a macro-scale through its position as the dominant language of New Jersey in, among others, governmental and educational domains. Moreover, this value trickles into local-situational contexts despite the emphasis on Portuguese and Spanish in the employees' home communities. As discussed extensively in the preceding chapter, capital is directly related to positive language ideologies (Darvin & Norton, 2015), including the valuation of English in these communities. It is also important to point out that some of Shine's employees envision English-language proficiency as a part of their own upwardly mobile trajectory. English language knowledge is certainly useful in the given setting. The analysis presented here, however, provides data that point to the existence of an alternative position.

Participation in intra-Shine communication relies on comprehension of Portuguese, and, while English potentially plays a role in employee-customer communication, it is mitigated through the possibility of contacting Magda for translation help. (See Chapter 3 for a more thorough description of Shine's language policy.) Indeed, as a part of a niche sector of the so-called 'ethnic economy' (Pécoud, 2010), employment at Shine is more dependent on Portuguese-language comprehension skills rather than English-language skills. Different jobs vary in terms of the amounts of language required to perform workplace tasks; moreover, language may be largely irrelevant to the daily realities of some professions (Gonçalves, 2020a; Gonçalves & Kelly-Holmes, 2021; Hovens, 2022; McAll, 2003; Piller & Lising, 2014; Serwe, 2021; Sherman & Homoláč, 2020; Sönderlundh & Keevalik, 2022; Strömmer, 2021). For Shine employees who clean empty houses, this point is highly salient, and, in this way, provides a space for Lusophone employees with minimal English-language resources to fully function within the local labor market.

For other employees like Adriana who are specifically deployed to new customers' houses to cultivate a positive early impression of Shine, however, effective communication with Anglophone monolinguals is essential. For this reason, it is noteworthy that highly effective communication is achieved in the absence of highly developed English-language communicative competence. The above discussion, thus, brings into focus the important role that objects, gestures and technology play in both supporting linguistic resources and substituting for them. In their flexible deployment of these resources, employees like Adriana achieve upward mobility (both in terms of the workplace hierarchy and material wealth) in the current capitalist era that emphasizes communication skills, suggesting that English-language competence – closely reflecting Blommaert in Sherris and Adami (2019) – represents only one possible component. In line with conclusions presented in one strand of the workplace communication literature (cf. Kirilova, 2017; Lockwood *et al.*, 2016), these findings emphasize the importance of conceptualizing communication ability as a broader set of skills than mere dominant-language proficiency.

5.7 Chapter Summary

Set in English-dominant households in which Lusophone domestic workers interact with their Anglophone customers, this chapter investigates the skillful deployment of communicative resources without reliance on knowledge of a shared language. By considering the sociolinguistic implications of these semiotic assemblages (Pennycook, 2017), this analysis reflects the recent focus in sociolinguistics on embodied communication (Bucholtz & Hall, 2016), semiotic repertoires (Kusters, 2021; Kusters *et al.*, 2017) and post-humanist applied linguistics (Pennycook, 2018). In this domain, investment in English is secondary to achieving mutual understanding through the tools available to the interlocutors. With respect to other workplace studies of multilingual employees in Anglophone North America, this work reflects the emphasis on multimodality discussed in Kleifgen (2013), but, as mentioned in the previous chapter, does not share its observations about the predominance of English as a lingua franca. This distinction highlights a key difference between blue-collar and white-collar settings, which has been supported by other blue-collar workplace settings, including Goldstein (1997); Sherman and Homoláč (2020); and chapters in Gonçalves and Kelly-Holmes (2021). As these findings are grounded in small-scale studies of language at work, additional research is needed to understand the extent of their agreement with larger trends. In this way, they could serve as a basis for similar studies to be carried out in different domestic work contexts across various cultural-linguistic settings to address the relevance of communication as a far broader concept than just language. This work will prove especially important when considering the larger influence of generative AI on communication in blue-collar workplace settings that do not rely on face-to-face interaction.

6 Conclusion

6.1 Communication Practices at a Migrant-Run, Multilingual Blue-Collar Workplace: Reflections on Emergent Themes and their Contributions to the Literature

Contextualized as part of the sociolinguistic strand on language, migration and domestic labor, this book has taken a deep ethnographic dive into both company-internal and company-external communication practices at a Portuguese-centric cleaning company that serves a primarily Anglophone clientele. Questions about power, its relationship to English-language proficiency and social mobility in an English-dominant setting guided our initial investigation into Shine in 2011. Identified by Heller (2010) as a fertile site for such investigations, the tertiary sector featured prominently within the growing literature on this topic at the time. Blue-collar workplaces' underrepresentation within this literature – with their heightened tendency for more extreme power asymmetries and display of underlying class divisions (Gonçalves, 2020a; Gonçalves & Kelly-Holmes, 2021; Gonçalves & Schluter, 2017; Lønsmann & Kraft, 2017) – suggested that they, too, merited further research attention. Moreover, the massive mobility of female workers to supply the global care chain (Gonçalves & Schluter, 2020; Ladegaard, 2020; Romero *et al.*, 2014) that is rendered less visible due to the informal domains in which many of these migrants work (McDowell & Dyson, 2011) enhanced the potential importance of exploring the communication dynamics at Shine as part of this macro-scale phenomenon. Indeed, the findings presented in the preceding chapters indicate some key deviations from those commonly highlighted in white-collar workplaces, contributing to a more comprehensive picture of workplace communication practices, which have, with some exceptions (Cf. Duchêne, 2009; Duchêne *et al.*, 2013; Gonçalves, 2020; Gonçalves & Kelly-Holmes, 2021; Gonçalves & Schluter, 2020; Handford & Matous, 2015; Heller, 2002; Hovens, 2020, 2021, 2022; Kaiper-Marquez & Makoni, 2022; Kraft, 2019; Lønsmann & Kraft, 2017; Pennycook & Otsuji, 2015; Piller & Lising, 2014; Schneider, 2018; Söderlundh & Keevallik, 2022; Sunaoshi, 2005; Thurlow, 2023) come from white-collar research sites. The following discussion will further detail such contributions of this project to the language and workplace literature, especially as it relates to blue-collar workplaces.

6.1.1 Methodological considerations and contributions

The scope of our understanding of Shine's communicative practices grew as our familiarity with the diverse voices of Shine deepened: a keen interest in more accurately conceptualizing new discoveries and disentangling apparent contradictions stimulated a series of follow-up discussions with Magda and other participants over the years. The preceding chapters of this book use content and discourse analysis as dual analytical tools through which to develop prominent themes that have emerged through this nearly decade-long research inquiry. Chapter 2 presents a comprehensive look at the approach employed in this study as part of a larger discussion about ethnographic methods. In line with the tendency for ethnographies to employ a more strategic and systemic approach to data collection subsequent to an initial exploratory phase (Johnstone, 2000), Kellie's long-time observations of Shine, brief employment at the company, sustained contact with its owner and employees and occasional participation in this community of practice provided the foundation and impetus for a more structured investigation that included both Kellie and Anne. Through its incorporation of observation, shadowing, document analysis and interviews, this more formal phase of data collection employed common ethnographic data collection tools; however, our ability to observe a wide-ranging spectrum of professional and private interactions – in conjunction with our personal engagement with many of Shine's employees during interviews – yielded uncommonly rich data.

The abundance of these data stems from our relatively unrestricted access to Shine-related domains. This point draws attention to the important role of our positionalities, both with respect to data collection and interpretation. Our insider status, especially that of Kellie, proved essential to establishing the high degree of interviewer-interviewee trust that enhanced the comprehensiveness of Shine employees' interview contributions and allowed us to conduct follow-up interviews as themes emerged during our analysis. At the same time, participants' perceptions of us were likely informed by their knowledge of our ties to Magda and, in this way, accounted for interview data that featured few critical comments about her. Cited as a common challenge to conducting research in blue-collar workplaces (Gonçalves, 2020; Lønsmann & Kraft, 2017), the inability of researchers to disassociate themselves from the supervisor who grants them access to the workplace/research site was magnified in this study by Kellie's pre-existing familial relationship with Magda, the participants' employer.

Partially informed by Kellie's long-standing engagement with the company, interpretations of the data, too, cannot be extricated from our positionalities. While it is true that Anne's participation in the project helped to mitigate some of this bias by including a more critically distant perspective, she, too, benefited from the ability to consult with Magda or Kellie whenever analysis benefited from a deeper understanding of background information. As a result, the preceding chapters do not present customers' and employees' voices in a balanced way. Instead, the disproportionate focus placed on Magda and her employees in the preceding chapters (rather than Shine's customers) reflects our greater capacity to triangulate the data from these sources despite the almost equal number of interviews with customers (N=20) vs. employees and employees' language brokers (N=21). These observations bring to the fore our alignment with existing literature that emphasizes researchers' findings as a product of their cultural frames and position (Hua, 2020; Martin-Jones & Martin, 2017; Schluter, 2020; Sorrells, 2016). In line with the tenets of ethnographic research, the analysis presented here represents one piece of a much larger picture that, given the researchers' differing relationships to the research site and its participants, is specific to the researchers themselves.

As discussed above, such a positionality allows researchers to tap into the trust that comes out of their familiarity with participants, and this trust helps to improve the quality of the resulting interviews. As beneficiaries of this trust, researchers also carry responsibility, especially with respect to Shine's employees from vulnerable populations. Discerning the line between the well-intentioned vs. exploitative dissemination of marginalized voices requires a critical reflection on the potential risks and benefits of the research. Table 2.1 in Chapter 2 provides insights into these risks and benefits as they relate specifically to this project. Consideration of these potential outcomes directly informs the 'key factors' in Figure 1.3 that appears in Chapter 1. While extensive access to the research site has resulted in an abundance of high-quality material that could provide the basis for an entire book series dedicated to communication practices at Shine, a sustained awareness of our positionalities and biases has tempered our interpretations of the data, providing the foundation for a written product that does not overstate its capacity to represent the different voices of participants. The result is an in-depth, well-supported addition to the literature that both advocates for the protection of a vulnerable population and presents its members as agentive, three-dimensional individuals.

6.2 English, Intercultural Competence, Language Policy, Power, Diasporic Belonging, Migrant Entrepreneurship and the Decentering of Language

6.2.1 English, power and the important role of multicompetence

As investigating the place of English at Shine represents an important focal point of the larger research project, Magda's highly developed English-language communicative competence – responsible for her ability to serve as the primary language broker between Shine's Anglophone customers and its Lusophone/Hispanophone employees – received considerable attention in our analysis. The extent to which employees rely on Magda's brokering to aid their communication with customers differs according to their levels of confidence in their English-language knowledge and, in the absence of this knowledge, their accommodation skills. For the employees who cannot deploy these skills, Magda – through her language brokering activities – closely monitors their interactions with customers. This resulting micromanagement demonstrates a way in which proficiency in the dominant language, building off of Max Weber's notion of legitimate domination, serves as a form of legitimated domination (Grillo, 1989). Given the prominence of English with respect to linguistic entrepreneurship (DeCosta et al., 2016) and the self-made speaker paradigm (Martín Rojo, 2018), this link between English-language knowledge and power is not surprising. At the same time, the potential for highly developed accommodation skills to compensate for the absence of overlapping linguistic resources between customers and employees adds nuance to this finding and merits further attention. This attention comes in the form of Chapter 5's in-depth exploration of this theme as integral to employees' multicompetence.

In these ways, Chapter 3 contributes to the literature on English-language proficiency and power in multilingual, US-based workplaces that employ migrants. The analysis of some Portuguese employees' reliance on Magda as a language broker – such as that of Paloma in Extract (16) of Chapter 3 – highlights connections between language ability and power in certain cases; however, the subsequent analysis places a big asterisk next to this finding. Employees who demonstrate well-honed accommodation skills achieve higher levels of autonomy from Magda than their counterparts who lack these skills. The emphasis these findings place on accommodation skills - rather than English-language proficiency – erodes a simplistic understanding of the relationship between language and power.

6.2.2 Shine's language policy, power and their relationship to accommodation and intercultural competence

While an interest in analyzing English-language proficiency and power preceded (and inspired) our study of Shine, a view from inside the company also underlined the importance of Magda's multilingual competence and emotional intelligence as components of her successful managerial style. Contact with Shine's employees highlighted potential communication difficulties between speakers of different languages and varieties, some combinations of which are not mutually intelligible (See Chapter 4, Section 4.4 for a more complete discussion about mutual intelligibility between standard varieties of Spanish and Portuguese). Individual employees' differing linguistic knowledge and accommodation skills contribute to their variable abilities to communicate with their co-workers from different language backgrounds. For pairings of employees that present communication difficulties, Magda engages in inter-employee brokering. One predictable example of this activity involves Magda's mediation to ensure that Shine's Hispanophone employees can effectively navigate the company's Portuguese-centric language policy. With deeper investigation into Magda's inter-employee brokering, a less clearly predictable example also emerges: the mediation between European and Brazilian Lusophone employees. While these employees can achieve a large degree of mutual intelligibility by slowing down their speaking rate and using more careful pronunciation, a lack of intercultural awareness, nevertheless, may lead to misunderstanding and, as Extract (13) from Chapter 3 indicates, even offense. Magda attempts to mitigate these potential misunderstandings by informing her Brazilian employees about key vocabulary and intonation patterns of European Portuguese varieties that Brazilian Lusophones may perceive as impolite. The choice to raise this topic only with Brazilian employees is noteworthy: it suggests that unidirectional intercultural communicative competence – whereby Brazilian staff undertake the work of adapting their perception to suit European Portuguese norms rather than Portuguese staff modifying their language to avoid offending Brazilian co-workers – is sufficient for promoting harmonious work relations. In this way, Magda's approach demonstrates her alignment with Shine's European Portuguese-centric orientation. As convergence to the norms of a given variety indicates its greater symbolic power over other locally present varieties (Bourhis, 1991), the insights from this chapter add to the research on language policies as 'mechanisms of power'(Johnson & Ricento, 2013: 12). Within this context, it expands findings from a sector of a North American blue-collar workplace – with its links between Portuguese-language comprehension/communicative competence and the cultivation of relationships with co-workers (Goldstein, 1997) – to company-wide internal communication.

6.3 Magda: A Complex Portrait of a Powerful, Emotionally Intelligent Migrant Entrepreneur

Magda's lack of favoritism toward employees who share her ethnolinguistic origins indicates her ability to achieve distance from existing biases toward her own culture. Moreover, as a Brazilian migrant who has had considerable contact with the local Portuguese community in both personal and professional contexts, Magda is well-positioned to identify linguistic differences between European and Brazilian Portuguese varieties that potentially contribute to Brazilians' misunderstanding. Through her ability to 'establish relationships and manage dysfunctions', Magda, thus, qualifies as an effective intercultural communicator (Byram, 1997: 38). Moreover, her development as an intercultural communicator is firmly grounded in her own experiences, a point that justifies Chapter 3's comprehensive coverage of Magda's life prior to establishing Shine.

Reflecting both Magda's oversized influence over Shine and our unfettered access to her, Chapter 3 – the longest chapter of this book – is devoted entirely to Magda and the characteristics that define her management style. Magda is a complex figure, and this chapter unpacks this complexity. On the one hand, Magda's classification of herself as a very 'demanding' person (Chapter 1, Extract (1)) directly aligns with our existing understanding of her as Shine's dominant figure who expresses her agentive voice through, among other means, the use of direct language. In one interview with us, her boast that she 'can fire anyone [she] want[s] to just because [she] do[es]n't like what they're wearing' suggests that she both recognizes and exploits her power over her employees. On the other hand, Shine's very low turnover rate and, in cases of position openings, the high number of applicants indicate that Magda does not frequently tap into this power to dismiss her employees on a whim. While it is true that one assistant manager describes Magda as 'not an easy person to work with', it is also important to consider her choice to remain as a full-time Shine employee until her retirement after 20 years with the company. It is also noteworthy that this employee returned to Shine in a part-time capacity following her retirement as a means of overcoming the monotony of retired life. As mentioned above, our perceived association with Magda likely discouraged interviewees from openly criticizing her. At the same time, our positionalities do not account for the unsolicited, extremely positive remarks of some participants, including one who 'thanks God for bringing Magda into [her] life' (from interview comments by Nina, discussed in Chapter 4). A multifaceted picture, thus, emerges of a company leader who demonstrates no attempts to mitigate her power but who, simultaneously, inspires long-time loyalty among those over whom she wields this power.

Magda's status as a minority throughout her formative years in terms of both social class (as a financially disadvantaged student at an expensive boarding school) and, later, cultural and linguistic background (as a Brazilian migrant to the US) fostered her keen self-awareness with respect to her sociocultural environment. Her social skills evolved along a similar trajectory: independence from her family at the age of seven required Magda, from a very early age, to learn to build relationships with those who shared neither her familial nor socioeconomic background. Equipped with these skills, Magda later felt comfortable migrating to the US, a setting in which her capacity to create connections across socioeconomic divides expanded to include relationships that spanned linguistic and cultural divides. These characteristics – namely self-awareness and social skills – represent two of the three primary traits of emotional intelligence (Goleman, 1998, 2000, 2015), a key to understanding Magda's successful communication both as the primary representative of Shine and as supervisor of the company's employees.

The third trait of emotional intelligence, empathy, deserves special attention because it functions as a central component of a company culture that trickles down to employees' behavior. Magda's empathy toward her employees becomes apparent through her decision to terminate Shine's services in reaction to a customer's insults to her cleaning staff (outlined in Extract (21) of Chapter 3). By 'providing cover from above' (Sinek, 2014: 8), Magda uses her power to defend her considerably less powerful employees. Based on interview comments from Lila (in Extract (4) of Chapter 4), a Hispanophone employee from Ecuador, a deeply empathetic approach also guides Shine employees' relations. Lila cites the caring mentorship of less experienced co-workers by members of Shine's core community of practice as a special characteristic of Shine that sets it apart from the local cleaning companies that primarily employ Hispanophone workers. This preference for the Shine community of practice further provides a foundation for the exploration of Hispanophone employees' positionality as part of the greater Ironbound community featured in Chapter 4. Magda's modeling of empathy from the top of Shine's hierarchy underlines its value as part of the company culture, which, as the extract from Lila shows, also characterizes much of company-internal communication. This empathy, together with Magda's self-awareness and social skills, points to her high level of emotional intelligence, a characteristic that helps to account for her admittedly demanding, no-nonsense approach on the one hand vs. her employees' long-standing loyalty to the company and warm feelings toward her on the other hand. Migrant entrepreneurs have received attention in the literature for their intercultural competence that stems from attachments to different cultural contexts, allowing them to adapt services and products from a foreign market to suit the demands of a domestic clientele (Cf. Rana & Elo, 2017). Rarely has this work devoted as extensive attention to these individuals as that given to Magda in this book. Drawing on nearly unfettered access to Magda over a period that exceeds a decade, Chapter 3's analysis of her complex personality with respect to her approach to management provides a detailed, personal contribution to this work. Through this portrait, multiple connections between background, personality, experience, intercultural competence, communicative proficiency and Shine's success emerge. These connections provide a uniquely rich understanding of the complex factors that have helped to shape a successful migrant entrepreneur.

6.4 Hispanophone Employees' Fit within Shine and the Larger Portuguese-Centric Ironbound Community: Observations about Investment and Implications for Language and Diaspora Research

Lila's reference to Shine's empathetic company culture in Chapter 3 provides insight into her motivation for working at Shine instead of Hispanophone-dominant employment alternatives. Chapter 4 broadens the scope of this insight by centering analysis on Shine's four Hispanophone employees, their preference for participation within the Shine community of practice, and their orientation to the larger Ironbound-based, Portuguese-centric community. Chapter 4 discusses employees' varying abilities to accommodate to co-workers who possess different linguistic repertoires. Out of the different cultural and linguistic backgrounds represented at Shine, in fact, the only employees who show a very limited tendency to accommodate to co-workers come from the Ironbound-resident Portuguese cohort. Employees such as Dona Aura (whose interview extract appears in Extract (1) of Chapter 4) tend not to modify their speech when addressing Hispanophone Latina co-workers, nor do they recognize these speakers' accommodation efforts when directed at them. This erasure of linguistic work is indicative of a perspective that stems from these employees' positionality as members of the dominant group and, in this way, reflects the underlying power differences inherent to directions of accommodation (Stell & Dragojevic, 2017).

As power dynamics within communities of practice tend to reproduce the power structures of the settings in which they are embedded (Contu & Willmott, 2003), the discussion turns to these Hispanophone Latina employees' positionality within the greater Ironbound community, the culture from which Magda modeled Shine. A look at these participants' residential and social network choices shows evidence that employment at Shine represents one component of a larger tendency to orient to the local Portuguese-centric diaspora. The acquisition of Portuguese-language features to aid these participants' workplace communication is similarly situated: it comes out of participants' larger goal of fitting in with their Portuguese-dominant neighbors, friends and/or partners.

This orientation to Portuguese across various domains highlights the role of investment (Norton, 2000), a product of the capital, identity and ideology associated with the target language and community (Darvin & Norton, 2015). Indeed, the large number of Portuguese-owned businesses within the Ironbound demonstrates the long-established economic capital of this diaspora group. In order to access this economic capital, ties to members of this group can function as social capital, and knowledge of Portuguese becomes a source of cultural capital. These different forms of capital also inform ideology, which casts Portuguese varieties and cultures in a positive light. An outcome of exposure to this ideology includes the desire to participate in the Portuguese-centric community; Hispanophone Latinas' acquisition efforts enhance their capacity to realize their imagined identity (Norton, 2000, 2013) as members of this group. With the choice to invest in the language of a locally prominent diaspora group rather than that of the autochthonous, dominant culture, this case serves as an example of horizontal assimilation (Prashad, 2001), a phenomenon that, given the link between capital and investment, holds potential to become more prevalent with the growth of migrant-owned businesses and networks that have benefited from the current era's redistribution of capital (Sabaté i Dalmau, 2013). These findings suggest that the process of decapitalization, or the loss of capital associated with a given language (Martín Rojo, 2013; Moyer, 2018), applies differently to different migration contexts. For the purposes of the larger study, it is noteworthy that the ability to orient to Portuguese serves as a valuable resource despite Shine's English-dominant regional setting. In these ways, the analysis presented in Chapter 4 contributes to the research strands in sociolinguistics that advocate for an expansion of the conceptualization of diasporic positionality (Cf. Albury & Schluter, 2021, special issue devoted to the topic) as well as the traditionally binary categorization of migrants vs. locals (Vigouroux, 2013). Furthermore, it extends the work on the interplay between identity, ideology and capital – the three interdependent components of investment (Darvin & Norton, 2015) – beyond the bounds of language acquisition studies.

6.4.1 Language proficiency as only one type of communicative resource for the agentive domestic worker

With the enhanced role of Portuguese discussed in Chapter 4, English takes on a less prominent role. While competence in Portuguese facilitates Shine-internal and community-directed communication, the utility of this language diminishes in the context of employees' interactions with Anglophone customers. Chapter 5 directly addresses this issue by detailing the diverse means through which these interlocutors achieve communication. This analysis also allows for some reflection on the research project's larger question about language proficiency for Shine employees.

In contrast to Lorente (2012, 2017) whose study of Filipina supermaids emphasizes the instrumentality of English-language proficiency, our findings from Shine point to the important role of multicompetence (Cook, 1991, 2016) for effective communication in domestic work contexts. Indeed, the ability to use objects, gestures and digital technologies to express an intended meaning – in a given space and in collaboration with a cooperative interlocutor – drives communication success. Participants vary according to their levels of multicompetence, but they can, nevertheless, benefit from incorporating multimodal communication practices (like placing a cleaning product on a napkin to alert the customer to the need to replace it) that carry pre-established meanings within the given community of practice. This focus on extra-linguistic resources aligns with the recent literature on translanguaging (Li, 2018); moreover, communicators' creative negotiation of meaning through the resources at their disposal reflects the agentive vision of the communicator underscored in post-humanist applied linguistics (Pennycook, 2018). In these ways, this chapter provides evidence to support the recent work on language as 'one of many resources deployed in social interaction'

(Blommaert in Sherris & Adami, 2019: 24). Accordingly, it contributes to the literature that envisions communication as a superordinate category, and linguistic resources, one of its sub-categories. This decentering of language also corresponds with the growing importance of translation technologies which de-emphasize the importance of interlocutors' shared linguistic repertoire through their ability to complement and augment participants' existing capacities to express their intended meaning.

Each of the aspects of multicompetence discussed in this chapter, in fact, diminishes the role of English-language proficiency in customer-employee interactions. As a primary aim of this research project included analysis of the language practices of Shine as a means of evaluating the place of English within a specific US-based workplace, the following discussion addresses this theme as it relates to each of the chapters' findings.

6.5 Insights into the Importance of English Based on Findings from the Shine Context

With its focus on English-language proficiency as a fundamental component of Magda's language brokering, Chapter 3 highlights a deep connection between English and power in the form of legitimated domination (Grillo, 1989). While this finding reflects expectations from the literature on the dominance of English (Cf. De Swaan, 2001), a full understanding of this finding also entails consideration of other important factors, including Magda's already-dominant position within the company's hierarchy. In terms of employees' levels of reliance and, as such, potential to be micromanaged through Magda's language brokering skills, our analysis finds various instances in which English-language competence does not predict the likelihood that Magda will receive a call to help mediate customer-employee communication. Instead, individual employees' capacity to accommodate to speakers from other language backgrounds represents a more reliable predictor of Magda's intervention and resulting oversight. In this way, Chapter 3 highlights the importance of English in the context of Magda's managerial role, but, as pointed out in the previous section, it simultaneously underlines the potential for accommodation skills to allow employees to maintain some power to act independently of Magda.

Of the Shine employees who have developed their ability to accommodate to speakers with different linguistic repertoires, the company's four Hispanophone Latina employees, whose daily interactions with their Lusophone co-workers require frequent accommodation work, qualify as noteworthy members of this group. Chapter 4 details the form of this accommodation work as a means of orienting to a Portuguese-centric community of practice and the larger Ironbound-based community in which it is embedded. As migrants to an English-dominant region and employees who serve Anglophone customers, their focus on the language and culture of a different migrant group – demonstrative of a lack of focused concentration on English – merits attention. Undergoing a lower degree of decapitalization than predicted by the literature (Martín Rojo, 2013; Moyer, 2018), Portuguese takes on some of the prestige that has traditionally been reserved for English. In this way, these findings underline the diminished status of English for these participants within this context.

Chapters 3 and 4 both discuss accommodation skills and strategies. Chapter 5 moves beyond the strictly linguistic realm of accommodation to include analysis of other means through which successful communication occurs between interlocutors who do not share linguistic repertoires. In doing so, the analysis foregrounds alternatives to shared English-language competence between customers and employers. In addition to accommodation skills, multicompetence (Cook, 1991, 2016) emerges as a key proficiency that informs successful extra-linguistic communication. While some employees consider their English-language competence as an impediment to their successful communication with customers, the case of Adriana, one of Shine's two assistant managers, presents a very different perspective. With her well-developed multicompetence that incorporates various embodied and multimodal strategies, she disregards English-speaking ability as an essential component for customer-employee communication. The lexical and syntactic components of English, which can easily be accessed if necessary through translation devices, are of secondary importance. Chapter 5, thus, expands the scope of Chapter 3's findings about accommodation skills to include multicompetence and multimodality as viable means through which successful communication takes place in the absence of fluent English-medium interaction. The ability of an employee like Adriana – who rates her English-language competence as 'poor' – to rise to the number two position at Shine and serve as the public face of Shine's domestic workers provides a rebuttal to studies (cf. Laitin & Reich, 2003) that correlate English-language proficiency with employability and upward mobility in the US.

English certainly retains its prominence as the regionally and nationally dominant language that, among many other functions, allows migrants greater access to the mechanisms of naturalization and legitimization; however, the sum of the analyses presented in the preceding chapters provides evidence that challenges the language's hegemonic status within the given context. In particular, it advocates for a nuanced perspective that considers accommodation skills and multicompetence as resources that offset individuals' reliance on English-language proficiency. These findings are noteworthy given the intersection of the international, national and regional scales that theoretically cement the prestigious status of English within Shine's northern New Jersey setting.

In line with this study's ethnographic approach, the conclusions presented in the pages of the preceding chapters cannot be removed from the Shine setting and, therefore, do not lend themselves to generalization. While such time-space constraints apply across studies of linguistic anthropology and qualitative sociolinguistics, they are particularly salient to Shine. Indeed, Section 6.6 (below), which provides an update on Shine and its employees at the time of publication, helps to underscore the finite character of both Shine as a cleaning company and the communicative practices of its employees.

6.6 The Status of Shine Today

Some major changes have taken place since our last data collection trip to Shine, and, as we finish writing up this book manuscript in the summer of 2023, a brief update and some closing reflections are in order. In 2019, Magda (aged 74) made the difficult decision to retire. Although she had been pondering her exit strategy for at least five years prior to her retirement, the potential impacts of this decision on her staff had weighed on her heavily and caused her to postpone executing her plan at various times. These postponements provide additional evidence of the symbiotic relationship between employees' years of loyal service to Shine and Magda's deep commitment to them. Rather than trying to sell her business, Magda agreed to let interested employees and customers maintain their cleaning services and relationships without Shine's mediation. According to this arrangement, customers could choose to employ their regularly scheduled cleaning lady directly, a choice that would also allow Shines' staff to maintain their jobs in a freelancing capacity. As a way of easing this transition, Magda spent the year preceding her retirement discussing her plan with her customers and employees. This advanced notice provided customers with some time to reflect on their preference for either committing to the new arrangement or seeking cleaning services through other means. Shine's employees, too, benefitted from this time as an opportunity to evaluate their options and identify their own post-Shine employment trajectories.

In a recent interview with Magda, she commented that her announcement to close Shine resulted in an overwhelming number of emails and phone calls from concerned customers in addition to calls and visits from distressed employees. In terms of Shine's customers, they demonstrated a wide range of perspectives on the best way to proceed. While some customers deemed the option of continuing with the same cleaning lady on a freelance basis to be acceptable, others felt uncomfortable hiring a self-employed domestic worker who was potentially undocumented, uninsured and unable to fully engage with them in English. For them, the hypothetical financial, sociopolitical and/or communicative risks were too high. Some of Shine's customers expressed high degrees of anxiety about this decision and 'begged' Magda to continue her business, noting that they had been loyal customers for over 30 years. One customer who accepted Shine's closure but wished to express her gratitude sent Magda a $1,000.00 thank you check for the excellent service that Shine had provided for her family over the years.

Similar to its customers, Shine's employees experienced the closure of Shine in a variety of ways. For those who relied heavily on Magda's coordination of their work duties, transportation, and/or language brokering, the closure instilled fears of losing all prospects of foreseeable employment in the US. According to Magda, one employee pointed out that she 'can't speak English' and had 'never been on a train or a bus', which led her to worry, 'How will I know how to reach customers' houses?' For other employees, especially drivers and assistant managers, the news was less daunting. Although they were not personally insured, they had already established comfortable communication with customers and familiarity with their routes from Newark to customers' houses. Shine's closure became an opportunity for self-employment, and, for those who chose to continue working together, cooperation at various levels. Some of these cooperative tasks include managing a weekly schedule with co-workers, devising workable transportation strategies to customers' houses and providing language brokering for certain employee-customer pairings.

As we worked on this manuscript, the communities in which Shine's employees operate were struggling with the outcomes of the pandemic. Fluctuating between 14.7% and 10.2% following the onset of the pandemic in the US in March 2020, the national unemployment rate reached its highest level since 1940 (Amadeo, August 7, 2020); moreover, estimates pointed to even higher rates among Latina women and migrants (Kochhar, June 9, 2020), two demographic categories that describe Shine's former employees. Indeed, the pandemic highlighted job security as a heightened concern for this group. Given the luxury status of household cleaning services for some customers and the relatively informal arrangement of their newly established cleaning agreements, the possibility of customers' abrupt termination of cleaning services cannot be underestimated, especially if a customer, too, faces unemployment. No longer able to count on Shine to reassign them to another house as needed, these workers' lack of affiliation with a cleaning company has rendered them more vulnerable to the impact of such circumstances. The unpredictability the future holds for their jobs, their finances and their economic survival carried considerable psychological and emotional distress, resonating with the experiences of other domestic workers in both national and international contexts (Cramer, 2020; Jordan & Dickerson, 2020; Land, 2020).

The altered perspective of the present-day setting provides a small snapshot of the new shape of employment for a group of migrant domestic workers who have recently become independent. To be clear, some of the new challenges they face are unrelated to communication. As alluded to above, the employment of an independent house cleaner comes with increased risk in terms of liability to the customers who can no longer rely on the company's insurance to pay for household items that may undergo damage during cleaning sessions. Moreover, workers' migration status undergoes greater scrutiny under this new arrangement as the onus of verifying documented status (and the potential repercussions of not verifying this status) is now transferred to the customers themselves. Undocumented status presents additional hurdles for the workers, including their lack of access to driver's licenses. As all of the customers' houses are located in suburbs that have extremely limited/no access to public transportation networks, this aspect of undocumented status severely complicates transportation to the customers' houses and, as such, access to the workplace.

6.7 Learning from Shine: Implications for Future Studies

Given this book's aims of addressing the place of English at a US-based domestic worker context, we return now to the implications of this new reality on communication. For some of Shine's former employees, the repercussions of losing Magda's 'cover from above' (Sinek, 2014) are daunting. This is especially the case for a portion of the Portuguese employees, like Paloma (discussed in Chapter 3) and Dona Aura (discussed in Chapter 4), who formed part of the core of Shine's community of practice. With their dependence on Magda for language brokering for company-external communication and reliance on Brazilian and Hispanophone Latina co-workers to undertake the accommodation work for company-internal communication, they did not develop the communication skills that would allow them to function as freelance workers. In addition to the lack of language brokering, the dissolution of the Shine community of practice also marks the slow deterioration of pre-established, non-linguistic ways to share/negotiate meaning (such as placing a cleaning product on a napkin to signal that the homeowner needs to purchase it) that were highlighted in the company's manual. While it is possible to build off these conventions that are familiar to both customers and employees, establishing new ones represents a more challenging task for workers who have, thus far, demonstrated little flexibility and multicompetence. This group of less flexible workers with limited multicompetence stands to lose the most from the new arrangement, and higher levels of English-language proficiency would certainly facilitate their communication with customers, potentially increasing the number of houses they serve. The instrumentality of English in this new domestic worker context, thus, aligns with previous work (Lorente, 2012, 2017) as well as more recent studies (Ben-Said, 2019; Kaiper, 2018; Kaiper-Marquez & Makoni, 2022; Rubdy & Pillai, 2022).

For the majority of Shine's employees, however, high levels of English-language proficiency are less relevant. The Hispanophone Latina and Brazilian workers who have honed their resourcefulness and accommodation skills while at Shine complement Portuguese workers like Adriana and Marta, who have developed these resources in their multilingual neighborhoods. Drawing on their experience in cleaning contexts with the same customers, they have become multicompetent communicators who deploy the various extra-linguistic strategies outlined in Chapter 5 to communicate with Anglophone customers. These are the same employees who have now assumed the responsibilities of coordinating schedules and transportation among their co-workers who continue to provide cleaning services for the same households. While Shine's closure exposes this group of workers to greater risk, it simultaneously increases their potential financial gain as Magda no longer collects any portion of the profits. Deviating from Lorente (2012, 2017) and aligning with Serwe (2021), this potential underlines the lack of correlation between proficiency in the dominant language and upward mobility. This group of employees is far more likely to demonstrate resilience in the face of employment hardships; their communicative resourcefulness is indicative of their larger approach to overcoming such challenges.

Although Shine no longer exists as a company, the findings presented here help to advance our understanding of communication in migrant domestic workplace settings with respect to researcher positionality, language policy, language brokering, migrant entrepreneurship, diasporic affiliations, accommodation, multicompetence and embodiment in the ways outlined in Section 6.1. Within the communication in the multilingual workplace literature, the lack of importance placed on English as a company lingua franca, among other characteristics, distinguishes it from much of the work on multilingual communication practices set in white-collar workplaces (Cf. Kleifgen, 2013) and even such blue-collar domestic work sites as the ones mentioned above (i.e Ben-Said, 2019; Kaiper-Marquez, 2022; Rubdy & Pillai, 2022). While a growing literature addresses such themes in a limited number of settings (Cf. Gonçalves & Kelly-Holmes, 2021; Hovens, 2022; Sherman & Homoláč, 2020; Sönderlundh & Keevalik, 2022), the sum of the research in this area remains insufficient for providing a comprehensive understanding of the big picture. Accordingly, the field will benefit from additional ethnographically grounded case study inquiries that are set within the diverse multilingual blue-collar workplaces across the various sociocultural contexts that exist globally.

References

Aguilar Jr, F.V. (2003) Global migrations, old forms of labor, and new transborder class relations. *Southeast Asian Studies* 41 (2), 137–161.
Ahearn, L.M. (2001) Language and agency. *Annual Reviews of Anthropology* 30, 109–137.
Albury, N.J. and Schluter, A.A. (2021) Reimagining language and belonging in the diaspora. *Lingua* 236. https://doi.org/10.1016/j.lingua.2021.103157.
Allott, N., Knight, C. and Smith, N. (eds) (2019) *The Responsibility of Intellectuals. Reflections by Noam Chomsky and Others after 50 Years*. London: University College London Press.
Amadeo, K. (2020) Unemployment rate by year since 1929 compared to inflation and GDP: U.S. unemployment rate history. *The Balance*, 7 August. See https://www.thebalance.com/unemployment-rate-by-year-3305506 (accessed 10 August 2020).
Anderson, B. (2001) *Doing the Dirty Work? The Global Politics of Domestic Labour*. London: Zed Books.
Androutsopoulos, J. (2006) Introduction: Sociolinguistics and computer-mediated communication. *Journal of Sociolinguistics* 10 (4), 419–438.
Androutsopoulos, J. (2021) Polymedia in interaction. *Pragmatics and Society* 12 (5), 707–724.
Angouri, J. (2014) Multilingualism in the workplace: Language practices in multilingual contexts. *Multilingua* 33 (1–2), 1–9.
Appadurai, A. (1996) *Modernity At Large: Cultural Dimensions of Globalization*. Minneapolis, MN: University of Minnesota Press.
Archer, M.S. (2000) *Being Human: The Problem of Agency*. Cambridge: Cambridge University Press.
Archer, M.S. (2007) *Making Our Way through the World: Human Reflexivity and Social Mobility*. Cambridge: Cambridge University Press.
Azevedo, M. (2005) *Portuguese: A Linguistic Introduction*. Cambridge: Cambridge University Press.
Barrett, R. (2006) Language ideology and racial inequality: Competing functions of Spanish in an Angloowned Mexican restaurant. *Language in Society* 35 (2), 163–204.
Baynam, M. (2013) Postscript. In A. Duchêne, M. Moyer and C. Roberts (eds) *Language, Migration and Social Inequalities: A Critical Sociolinguistic Perspective on Institutions and Work* (pp. 272–276). Bristol: Multilingual Matters.
Bell, A. (2014) *The Guidebook to Sociolinguistics*. Chichester: Wiley Blackwell.
Ben-Said, S. (2019) You speak English with your boss, but you speak Chinese with me! Constraints and possibilities in language use by Hong Kong foreign domestic helpers. *Tzu Chi University Journal of the Humanities and Social Science* 24, 65–106.
Ben-Said, S. (2022) Enacting power through control and surveillance: Narrative reflections from a Hong-Kong-based foreign domestic helper. *Journal of Postcolonial Linguistics* 7, 32–50.
Birdwhistell, R.L. (1970) *Kinesics and Context*. Philadelphia, PA: University of Pennsylvania Press.

Blackledge, A. and Creese, A. (2017) Translanguaging and the body. *International Journal of Multilingualism* 14 (3), 250–268.
Blackwood, R., Tufi, S. and Amos, W. (eds) (forthcoming) *The Bloomsbury Handbook of Linguistic Landscapes*. London: Bloomsbury.
Block, D. (2012) Unpicking agency in sociolinguistic research with migrants. In S. Gardner and M. Martin-Jones (eds) *Multilingualism, Discourse and Ethnography* (pp. 47–60). New York: Routledge.
Block, D. (2018) *Political Economy in Sociolinguistics: Neoliberalism, Inequality and Social Class*. London: Bloomsbury.
Block, D., Gray, J. and Holborow, M. (2012) *Neoliberalism and Applied Linguistics*. New York: Routledge.
Blommaert, J. (2010) *The Sociolinguistics of Globalization*. Cambridge: Cambridge University Press.
Blommaert, J., Collins, J. and Slembrouck, S. (2005) Spaces of multilingualism. *Language and Communication* 25, 197–216.
Boas, T. and Gans-Morse, J. (2009) Neoliberalism: From new liberal philosophy to anti-liberal slogan. *Studies in Comparative International Development* 44 (2), 137–161.
Bourdieu, P. (1991) *Language and Symbolic Power*. Cambridge, MA: Harvard University Press.
Bourdieu, P. (1986) The forms of capital. In J. Richardson (ed.) *Handbook of Theory and Research for the Sociology of Education* (pp. 241–258). New York, NY: Greenwood Press.
Bourdieu, P. (1977) *Outline of a Theory of Practice*. Cambridge: Cambridge University Press.
Bourdieu, P. and Wacquant, L.J.D. (1992) *An Invitation to Reflexive Sociology*. Chicago, IL: The University of Chicago Press.
Bourhis, R.Y. (1991) Organizational communication and accommodation: Toward some conceptual and empirical links. In H. Giles, J. Coupland and N. Coupland (eds) *Contexts of Accommodation* (pp. 270–303). Cambridge: Cambridge University Press.
Briggs, C.L. (1986) *Learning How to Ask: A Sociolinguistic Appraisal of the Role of the Interview in Social Science Research*. Cambridge: Cambridge University Press.
Brown, P. and Levinson, S.C. (1987) *Politeness: Some Universals in Language Usage*. Cambridge: Cambridge University Press.
Bucholtz, M. and Hall, K. (2016) Embodied sociolinguistics. In N. Coupland (ed.) *Sociolinguistics: Theoretical Debates* (pp. 173–197). Cambridge: Cambridge University Press.
Burcea, S.G. and Sabie, O.M. (2020) Is emotional intelligence a determinant factor for leader's skills development? Essential literature perspectives. *Management and Economics Review* 1, 68–77.
Byram, M. (1997) *Teaching and Assessing Intercultural Communicative Competence* (1st edn). Clevedon: Multilingual Matters.
Cambell, E. and Lassier, L.E. (2015) *Doing Ethnography Today: Theories, Methods and Exercises*. Oxford: Wiley Blackwell.
Cameron, D. (2000) Styling the worker: Gender and the commodification of language in the globalized service economy. *Journal of Sociolinguistics* 4 (3), 323–347.
Cameron, D. (2001) *Working with Spoken Discourse*. London: Sage Publications.
Cameron, D., Frazer, E., Harvey, P., Rampton, M.B.H. and Richardson, K. (1992) *Researching Language: Issues of Power and Method*. London: Routledge.
Campos, R., Zaimakis, Y. and Pavoni, A. (eds) (2021) *Political Graffiti in Critical Times: The Aesthetics of Street Politics*. New York: Berghahn.
Canagarajah, S. (2004) Subversive identities, pedagogical safe houses, and critical learning. In B. Norton and K. Toohey (eds) *Critical Pedagogies and Language Learning* (pp. 116–137). Cambridge: Cambridge University Press.
Canagarajah, S.A. (2013) *Literacy as Translingual Practice*. New York: Routledge.
Canagarajah, S. (2016) Shuttling between scales in the workplace: Reexamining policies and pedagogies for migrant professionals. *Linguistics and Education* 34, 47–57.

Canagarajah, S. (2017) *The Routledge Handbook of Migration and Language*. New York: Routledge.
Canagarajah, S. (2020) Transnational work, translingual practices, and interactional sociolinguistics. *Journal of Sociolinguistics* 24 (5), 555–573.
Canagarajah, S. (2021) Materialising semiotic repertoires: Challenges in the interactional analysis of multilingual communication. *International Journal of Multilingualism* 18 (2), 1–20.
Carling, J., Erdal, M.B. and Ezzati, R. (2014) Beyond the insider-outsider divide in migration research. *Migration Studies* 2 (1), 36–54.
Carter, R. and McCarthy, M. (2006) *Cambridge Grammar of English: A Comprehensive Guide*. Cambridge: Cambridge University Press.
Carvahlo, A.M. (2010) Portuguese in the USA. In K. Potowski (ed.) *Language Diversity in the USA* (pp. 223–237). Cambridge: Cambridge University Press.
Castles, S. (2013) The forces driving global migration. *Journal of Intercultural Studies* 34 (2), 122–140.
Cavanaugh, J.R. and Shankar, S. (2014) Producing authenticity in global capitalism: Language, materiality, and value. *American Anthropologist* 116 (1), 51–64.
Chan, Ka Wai, C. (2023) Two Filipina domestic helpers' intercultural competence at work. Unpublished Doctoral Thesis, Department of English and Communication, The Hong Kong Polytechnic University.
Chang, G. (2000) *Disposable Domestics: Immigrant Women Workers in the Global Economy*. Cambridge, MA: South End Press.
Chatterjee, A. and Schluter, A. (2020) "Maid to maiden": The false promise of English for the daughters of domestic workers in post-colonial Kolkata. *International Journal of the Sociology of Language* 262, 67–95.
Chomsky, N. (1967) The responsibility of intellectuals. *New York Review*, February. https://www.nybooks.com/articles/1967/02/23/a-special-supplement-the-responsibility-of-intelle/.
Coates, J. (1996) *Women Talk: Conversation between Women Friends*. Oxford: Blackwell.
Codó, E. (2013) Trade unions and NGOs under neoliberalism: Between regimenting migrants and subverting the state. In A. Duchêne, M. Moyer and C. Roberts (eds) *Language, Migration and Social Inequalities: A Critical Sociolinguistic Perspective on Institutions and Work* (pp. 25–55). Bristol: Multilingual Matters.
Conger, J.A. (2004) Developing leadership capability: What's inside the black box? *Academy of Management Executive* 18, 136–139.
Contu, A. and Willmott, H. (2003) Re-embedding situatedness: The importance of power relations in learning theory. *Organization Science* 14 (3), 283–296.
Cook, V. (1991) The poverty-of-the-stimulus argument and multicompetence. *Second Language Research* 7 (2), 103–117.
Cook, V. (2016) Premises of multicompetence. In V. Cook and Li Wei (eds) *The Cambridge Handbook of Linguistic Multicompetence* (pp. 1–25). Cambridge: Cambridge University Press.
Corona, R., Stevens, L.F., Halfond, R.W., Shaffer, C.M., Reid-Quinones, K. and Gonzalez, T. (2012) A qualitative analysis of what Latino parents and adolescents think and feel about language brokering. *Journal of Child and Family Studies* 21, 788–798.
Coulmas, F. (ed.) (1986) *Direct and Indirect Speech*. Berlin: Mouton de Gruyter.
Coupland, N. (ed.) (2010) *The Handbook of Language and Globalization*. Oxford: Wiley-Blackwell Publishing.
Coupland, N. (ed.) (2016) *Sociolinguistics: Theoretical Debates*. Cambridge: Cambridge University Press.
Cramer, M. (2020) A dilemma for some: Should you still hire a cleaner? *The New York Times*, 26 March. See https://www.nytimes.com/2020/03/26/us/coronavirus-house-cleaner.html?searchResultPosition=2 (accessed 26 March 2020).
Crawford, J. (1992) *Language Loyalties: A Source Book on the Official English Controversy*. Chicago, IL: The University of Chicago Press.

Curdt-Christiansen, X.L. (2018) Family language policy. In J.W. Tollefson and M. Pérez-Milans (eds) *Oxford Handbook of Language Policy and Planning* (pp. 420–441). Oxford: Oxford University Press.
Czarniawska, B. (2007) *Shadowing: And Other Techniques for Doing Fieldwork in Modern Societies*. Mâlmo: Copenhagen Business School Press.
Darvin, R. (2016) *The Routledge Handbook of Language and Identity*. New York: Routledge.
Darvin, R. and Norton, B. (2015) Identity and a model of investment in applied linguistics. *Annual Review of Applied Linguistics* 35, 36–56.
Dashti, A.A. (2013) Interacting with domestic workers in Kuwait: Grammatical features of foreigner talk. A case study. *International Journal of the Sociology of Language* 20 (224), 63–84.
De Costa, P.I. (2010) Language ideologies and standard English language policy in Singapore: Responses of a 'designer immigrant' student. *Language Policy* 9 (3), 217–239.
De Costa, P.I, Park, J. and Wee, L. (2016) Language learning as linguistic entrepreneurship: Implications for language education. *The Asia-Pacific Education Researcher* 25, 695–702.
De Costa, P.I., Park, J. and Wee, L. (2018) Linguistic entrepreneurship as affective regime: Organizations, audit culture, and second/foreign language education policy. *Language Policy* 18, 387–406.
De Costa, P.I., Park, J. and Wee, L. (2021) Why linguistic entrepreneurship? *Multilingua* 40 (2), 139–153.
De Swaan, A. (2001) *Words of the World: The Global Language System*. Cambridge: Polity Press.
DeFina, A. (2003) *Identity in Narrative: A Study of Immigrant Discourse*. Amsterdam: John Benjamins.
Del Torto, L.M. (2008) Once a broker, always a broker: Non-professional interpreting as identity accomplishment in multigenerational Italian-English bilingual family interaction. *Multilingua* 27, 77–97.
Denzin, N.K. (2001) *Interpretive Interactionism*. Thousand Oaks, CA: Sage Publications.
Deumert, A. and Mabandla, N. (2013) "Every day a new shop pops up": South Africa's 'new' Chinese diaspora and the multilingual transformation of rural towns. *English Today* 113 (29), 44–52.
Dirim, I. and Auer, P. (2012) *Türkisch Sprechen nicht nur die Türken: Über die Unschärfebeziehung zwischen Sprache und Ethnie in Deutschland*. [Not only Turks Speak Turkish: About the Fuzzy Relationship between Language and Ethnicity in Germany]. Berlin: De Gruyter.
Divita, D. (2014) Multilingualism and the lifespan: Case studies from a language course for Spanish seniors in Saint-Denis, France. *International Journal of Multilingualism* 11 (1), 1–22.
Divita, D. (2020) Domestic Spanish handbooks: Language and labor in the American home. *International Journal of the Sociology of Language* (262), 17–37.
Divita, D. (2021) Spanish *Bonnes* in 1960s Paris: Occupational narratives from transnational migrants in later life. In K. Gonçalves and H. Kelly-Holmes (eds) *Language, Global Mobilities, Blue-Collar Worker and Blue-Collar Workplaces* (pp. 91–106). New York: Routledge.
Duchêne, A. (2009) Marketing, management and performance: Multilingualism as commodity in a tourism call centre. *Language Policy* 8 (1), 27–50.
Duchêne, A. and Heller, M. (2012) *Language in Late Capitalism: Pride and Profit*. New York: Routledge.
Duchêne, A., Moyer, M. and Roberts, C. (2013) Introduction: Recasting institutions and work in multilingual and transnational spaces. In A. Duchêne, M. Moyer and C. Roberts (eds) *Language, Migration, and Social Inequalities: A Critical Sociolinguistic Perspective on Institutions and Work* (pp. 1–21). Bristol: Multilingual Matters.
Duff, P., Wong, P. and Early, M. (2000) Learning language for work and life: The linguistic socialization of immigrant Canadians seeking careers in healthcare. *Canadian Modern Language Review* 57 (1), 9–57.

Ferreira, L. and Holt, D.E. (2014) On the partially divergent phonology of Spanish, Portuguese and points in between. In P. Amaral and A.M. Carvalho (eds) *Portuguese-Spanish Interfaces: Diachrony, Synchrony, and Contact* (pp. 123–150). Amsterdam: John Benjamins Publishing Company.

Fincham, B., McGuinness, M. and Murray, L. (2010) *Mobile Methodologies*. Hampshire: Palgrave Macmillan.

Fine, M. (1994) Working the hyphens: Reinventing self and other in qualitative research. In N.K. Denzin and Y.S. Lincoln (eds) *Handbook of Qualitative Research* (pp. 70–82). Thousand Oaks, CA: Sage Publications.

Foucault, M. (1980) *Power/Knowledge: Selected Interviews and Other Writings by Michel Foucault*. New York: Pantheon.

Fuller, J.M. and Leeman, J. (2020) *Speaking Spanish in the US: The Sociopolitics of Language*. Bristol: Multilingual Matters.

Galloway, L., Kapasi, I. and Sang, K. (2015) Entrepreneurship, leadership, and the value of feminist approaches to understanding them. *Journal of Small Business Management* 53 (3), 683–692.

Gamper, M. (2015) Bourdieus Konzept des Sozialkapitals und seine Bedeutung die Migrationsforschung. [Bourdieu's concept of social capital and its meaning for migration research]. In J. Reuter and P. Mecheril (eds) *Schlusselwerke der Migrationsforschung. Pionierstudien und Referenztheorien*. [Key Works of Migration Research. Pioneering Studies and Referential Theories] (pp. 343–360). Wiesbaden: Springer.

García, O. and Li, W. (2014) *Translanguaging: Language, Bilingualism and Education*. London: Palgrave Pivot.

García, O., Flores, N. and Spotti, M. (eds) (2017) *The Oxford Handbook of Language and Society*. Oxford: Oxford University Press.

Giddens, A. (1984) *The Constitution of Society*. Cambridge: Polity Press.

Giddens, A. (2003) *Runaway World: How Globalisation is Reshaping Our World*. New York: Routledge.

Gilder, G. (1986) Jobs: Women in the Workforce. *The Atlantic*, Septmber. https://www.theatlantic.com/magazine/archive/1986/09/jobs-women-in-the-work-force/667374/.

Goffman, E. (1957) Alienation from Interaction. *Human Relations* 10 (1), 47–60.

Goffman, E. (1959) *The Presentation of Self in Everyday Life*. London: Penguin Books.

Gogia, N. (2006) Unpacking corporeal mobilities: The global voyages of labour and leisure. *Environment and Planning* 38, 359–375.

Goldstein, T. (1997) *Two Languages at Work: Bilingual Life on the Production Floor*. New York: Mouton de Gruyter.

Goleman, D. (1998) What makes a leader? *Harvard Business Review*, 93–102.

Goleman, D. (2000) *Emotional Intelligence: Why it Can Matter More than IQ*. London: Bloomsbury.

Goleman, D. (2015) What makes a leader? On emotional intelligence. *Harvard Business Review*, 1–21.

Gonçalves, K. (2012) The semiotic landscapes and the discourses of place within a Portuguese-speaking neighborhood. *Interdisciplinary Journal of Portuguese Diaspora Studies* 1, 71–99.

Gonçalves, K. (2013) *Conversations of Intercultural Couples*. Berlin: Mouton de Gruyter.

Gonçalves, K. (2015) The pedagogical implications of ELF in a domestic migrant workplace. In H. Bowles and A. Cogo (eds) *International Perspectives on English as a Lingua Franca* (pp. 136–158). Houndmills: Palgrave MacMillan.

Gonçalves, K. (2020a) "What the fuck is this for a language, this cannot be Deutsch?": Language ideologies, policies, and semiotic practices of a kitchen crew in a hotel restaurant. *Language Policy* 19, 417–441.

Gonçalves, K. (2020b) *Labour Policies, Language Use and the 'New' Economy: The Case of Adventure Tourism*. Cham: Palgrave Macmillan.

Gonçalves, K. (2022) "I need her more than she needs me": An intersectional approach to privilege, marginalization and power asymmetries within a Brazilian domestic labor context. *Journal of Post-Colonial Linguistics* 7, 13–31.

Gonçalves, K. and Schluter, A. (2017) Please do not leave any notes for the cleaning lady, as many do not speak English fluently: Policy, power and language brokering in a multilingual workplace. *Language Policy* 16, 241–265.

Gonçalves, K. and Schluter, A. (2020) Introduction: Language, inequality and global care work. *The International Journal of the Sociology of Language* 262, 1–16.

Gonçalves, K. and Kelly-Holmes, H. (eds) (2021) *Language, Global Mobilities and Blue-collar Workplaces*. New York: Routledge.

Gonçalves, K. and Lanza, E. (forthcoming) Expanding the LL: Familyscapes, multilingualism, and family language policy. In R. Blackwood, S. Tufi and W. Amos (eds) *The Bloomsbury Handbook of Linguistic Landscapes*. London: Bloomsbury.

Goodwin, C. (2000) Action and embodiment within situated human interaction. *Journal of Pragmatics* 32, 1489–1522.

Grillo, R.D. (1989) *Dominant Languages: Language and Hierarchy in Britain and France*. Cambridge: Cambridge University Press.

Guinto, N. (2019) The place/s of Tagalog in Hong Kong's central district: Negotiating center-periphery dynamics. *Linguistic Landscape* 5 (2), 160–178.

Gumperz, J. (1982) *Discourse Strategies*. Cambridge: Cambridge University Press.

Habermas, J. (1971) *Knowledge and Human Interests* (trans. J.J. Shapiro). Boston: Beacon Press.

Handford, M. and Matous, P. (2015) Problem-solving discourse on an international construction site: Patterns and practices. *English for Specific Purposes* 38, 85–98.

Heller, M. (2002) *Éléments d'une sociolinguistique critique*. Paris: Didier.

Heller, M. (2003) Globalization, the new economy, and the commodification of language and identity. *Journal of Sociolinguistics* 7 (4), 473–492.

Heller, M. (2008) Doing ethnography. In Li Wei and M.G. Moyer (eds) *Research Methods in Bilingualism and Multilingualism* (pp. 249–262). Oxford: Blackwell.

Heller, M. (2010) The commodification of language. *Annual Review of Anthropology* 39, 101–114.

Heller, M. (2011) *Paths to Post-Nationalism*. Oxford: Oxford University Press.

Heller, M. and McElhinny, B. (2017) *Language, Capitalism, Colonialism: Toward a Critical History*. Toronto: University of Toronto Press.

Heller, M., Pietikainen, S. and Pujolar, J. (2018) *Critical Sociolinguistic Methods: Studying Language Issues that Matter*. New York: Routledge.

Hochschild, A. (1989) *The Second Shift: Working Families and the Revolution at Home* (with A. Machung). New York: Penguin Books.

Hochschild, A.R. (2000) The global care chains and emotional surplus value. In W. Hutton and A. Giddens (eds) *On The Edge: Living with Global Capitalism* (pp. 130–146). London: Jonathan Cape.

Holmes, J., Marra, M. and Vine, B. (2011) *Leadership, Discourse and Ethnicity*. Oxford: Oxford University Press.

Hovens, D. (2020) Workplace learning through human-machine interaction in a transient multilingual blue-collar work environment. *Journal of Linguistic Anthropology* 30 (3), 369-388.

Hovens, D. (2021) Language policy and linguistic landscaping in a contemporary blue-collar workplace in the Dutch-German borderland. *Language Policy* 20 (4), 645–666.

Hovens, D. (2022) Breakdowns and assemblages: Including machine-actants in sociolinguistic ethnographies of blue-collar work environments. *Journal of Sociolinguistics* 27, 3–23.

Hua, Z. (2020) Making a stance: Social action for language and intercultural research. *Language and Intercultural Communication* 20 (2), 206–212.

Hua, Z. and Li, W. (2022) Translanguaging in performance or performance in translanguaging. *Journal of Multilingual and Multicultural Development*, 1–14.

Hua, Z., Li, W. and Lyons, A. (2017) Polish shop(ping) as translanguaging space. *Social Semiotics* 27 (4), 411–433.

Hubbard, B. and Donovan, L. (2020) Laid off and locked up: Virus traps domestic workers in Arab States. *New York Times*, 6 July. See https://www.nytimes.com/2020/07/06/world/middleeast/coronavirus-saudi-domestic-workers-maids-arab.html?searchResultPosition=2 (accessed 20 July 2021).

Hymes, D. (1974) *Foundations in Sociolinguistics: An Ethnographic Approach*. Philadelphia, PA: University of Pennsylvania Press.

International Labour Organization (2013) *Domestic Workers Across the World: Global and Regional Statistics and the Extent of Legal Protection*. Geneva: International Labour Organization.

International Labour Organization (2017) Implementation of international labour standards for domestic workers. *What Works Research Brief* 9.

Jacquemet, M. (2005) Transidiomatic practices: Language and power in the age of globalization. *Language and Communication* 25, 257–277.

Jacquemet, M. (2016) Transidioma. *Revista da Anpoll* 40, 19–32.

Johnson, D.C. and Ricento, T. (2013) Conceptual and theoretical perspectives in language planning and policy: Situating the ethnography of language policy. *International Journal of the Sociology of Language* 219, 7–21.

Johnstone, B. (2000) *Qualitative Methods in Sociolinguistics*. Oxford: Oxford University Press.

Johnstone, B. (2002) *Discourse Analysis*. Malden: Blackwell.

Jones, C.J. and Tricket, E.J. (2005) Immigrant adolescents behaving as culture brokers: A study of families from the former Soviet Union. *The Journal of Social Psychology* 145 (4), 405–428.

Jonsson, C. and Blåsjo, M. (2020) Translanguaging and multimodality in workplace texts and writing. *International Journal of Multilingualism* 17 (3), 361–381.

Jordan, M. and Dickerson, C. (2020) 'Plz cancel our cleaning': Virus leads many to cast aside household help. *The New York Times*, 25 March. See https://www.nytimes.com/2020/03/25/us/coronavirus-housekeepers-nannies-domestic-undocumented-immigrants.html?searchResultPosition=2 (accessed 25 March 2020).

Kaiper, A. (2018) "If you don't have English, you're just as good as a dead person": A narrative of adult English language literacy within post-apartheid South Africa. *International Review of Education* 64 (6), 737–757.

Kaiper-Marquez, A. (2022) Interstitial glimpses: The linguistic agency/oppression of South African domestic workers. *Journal of Postcolonial Linguistics* 7, 72–88.

Kaiper-Marquez, A. and Makoni, S. (2022) Special issue on global domestic workers. *Journal of Post-Colonial Linguistics* 7, 1–12.

Kirilova, M. (2017) 'Oh so it's a DANISH boyfriend you've got': Co-membership and cultural fluency in job interviews with minority background applicants in Denmark. In J. Angouri, M. Marra and J. Holmes (eds) *Negotiating Boundaries at Work* (pp. 22–49). Edinburgh: Edinburgh University Press.

Kleifgen, J.A. (2013) *Communicative Practices at Work: Multimodality and Learning in a High-Tech Firm*. Bristol: Multilingual Matters.

Kloosterman, R. and Rath, J. (2001) Immigrant entrepreneurs in advanced economies: Mixed embeddedness further explored. *Journal of Ethnic and Migration Studies* 27 (2), 189–201.

Kochhar, R. (2020) Hispanic women, immigrants, young adults, those with less education hit hardest by COVID-19 job losses. *The Pew Research Center*, 9 June. See https://www.pewresearch.org/fact-tank/2020/06/09/hispanic-women-immigrants-young-adults-those-with-less-education-hit-hardest-by-covid-19-job-losses/ (accessed 8 August 2020).

Kramsch, C. (2021) *Language as Symbolic Power*. Cambridge: Cambridge University Press.

Kress, G. (2009) *Multimodality: A Social Semiotic Approach to Contemporary Communication*. New York: Routledge.

Kusters, A. (2021) Introduction: The semiotic repertoire: Assemblages and evaluation of resources. *International Journal of Multilingualism* 18 (2), 183–189.

Kusters, A., Spotti, M., Swanwick, R. and Tapio, E. (2017) Beyond languages, beyond modalities: Transforming the study of semiotic repertoires. *International Journal of Multilingualism* 14 (3), 219–232.

Ladegaard, H.J. (2012) The discourse of powerlessness and repression: Identity construction in domestic helper narratives. *Journal of Sociolinguistics* 16, 450–482.

Ladegaard, H.J. (2013) Laughing at adversity: Laughter as communication in domestic helper narratives. *Journal of Language and Social Psychology* 32, 459–480.

Ladegaard, H.J. (2015) Crying as communication in domestic helper narratives: Towards a social psychology of crying in discourse. *Journal of Language and Social Psychology* 33, 579–605.

Ladegaard, H.J. (2017) *The Discourse of Powerlessness and Repression: Life Stories of Domestic Migrant Workers in Hong Kong.* London: Routledge.

Ladegaard, H.J. (2020) Language competence, identity construction and discursive boundary-making: Distancing and alignment in domestic migrant worker narratives. *The International Journal of the Sociology of Language* (262), 97–122.

Ladegaard, H.J. and Phipps, A. (2020) Intercultural research and social activism. *Language and Intercultural Communication* 20 (2), 67–80.

Laitin, D.D. and Reich, R. (2003) A liberal democratic approach to language justice. In W. Kymlicka and A. Patten (eds) *Language Rights and Political Theory* (pp. 80–140). Oxford: Oxford University Press.

Lan, P.C. (2006) *Global Cinderellas: Migrant Domestics and Newly Rich Employers in Taiwan.* Durham, NC: Duke University Press.

Lanza, E. (2008) Selecting individuals, groups and sites. In Li Wei and M.G. Moyer (eds) *Research Methods in Bilingualism and Multilingualism* (pp. 73–87). Oxford: Blackwell.

Lanza, E. (2021) The family as a space: Multilingual repertoires, language practices and lived experiences. *Journal of Multilingual and Multicultural Development* 42 (8), 763–771.

Lave, J. and Wenger, E. (1991) *Situated Learning: Legitimate Peripheral Participation.* Cambridge: Cambridge University Press.

Law, J. and Urry, J. (2004) Enacting the social. *Economy and Society* 33 (3), 390–410.

Lazarevic, V., Rafaelli, M. and Wiley, A. (2014) Language and non-linguistic brokering: Diversity of experiences of immigrant young adults from Eastern Europe. *Journal of Comparative Family Studies* 4, 517–535.

Lester, J.N. and Anders, A.D. (2018) Engaging ethics in postcritical ethnography: Troubling transparency, trustworthiness, and advocacy. *Forum Qualitative Sozialforschung / Forum: Qualitative Social Research* 19 (3–4), 1–19.

Levon, E. (2018) Ethnographic fieldwork. In C. Mallinson, B. Childs and G. Van Herk (eds) *Data Collection in Sociolinguistics: Methods and Applications* (2nd edn, pp. 85–106). London: Routledge.

Lexander, K.V. and Androutsopoulos, J. (2021) Working with mediagrams: A methodology for collaborative research on mediational repertoires in multilingual families. *Journal of Multilingual and Multicultural Development* 42 (1), 1–18.

Lexander, K.V. and Androutsopoulos, J. (2023) *Multilingual Families in a Digital Age: Mediational Repertoires and Transnational Practices.* New York: Routledge.

Li, C.N. (1986) Direct and indirect speech: A functional study. In F. Coulmas (ed.) *Direct and Indirect Speech* (pp. 29–45). Berlin: Mouton de Gruyter.

Li, W. (2018) Translanguaging as a practical theory of language. *Applied Linguistics* 39 (1), 9–35.

Light, I., Sabagh, G., Bozorgmehr, M. and Der-Martirosian, C. (1994) Beyond the ethnic enclave economy. *Social Problems* 41 (1), 65–80.

Lim, L., Stroud, C. and Wee, L. (eds) (2018) *The Multilingual Citizen: Towards a Politics of Language for Agency and Change.* Bristol: Multilingual Matters.

Lincoln, P.C. (1979) Dual lingualism: Passive bilingualism in action. *Te Reo* 22, 65–72.

Linde, C. (1993) *Life Stories: The Creation of Coherence.* Oxford: Oxford University Press.

Lindström, J.K., Norrby, C., Wide, C. and Nilsson, J. (2017) Intersubjectivity at the counter: Artefacts and multimodal interaction in theatre box office encounters. *Journal of Pragmatics* 108, 81–97.

Lockwood, J., Finch, S.J., Ryder, N., Gregorio, S., Dela Cruz, R., Cook, B. and Ramos, L. (2016) Dealing with angry western customers in Asian call centres: A cultural divide? In L. Pickering, E. Friginal and S. Staples (eds) *Talking at Work: Corpus-Based Explorations of Workplace Discourses* (pp. 155–178). London: Palgrave Macmillan.

Lønsmann, D. and Kraft, K. (2017) Language in blue-collar workplaces. In B. Vine (ed.) *The Routledge Handbook of Language in the Workplace* (pp. 138–150). New York: Routledge.

Lønsmann, D. and Mortensen, J. (2018) Language policy and social change: A critical examination of the implementation of an English-only language policy in a Danish company. *Language in Society* 47 (3), 435–456.

Lorente, B.P. (2010) Packaging English-speaking products: Maid agencies in Singapore. In H. Kelly-Holmes and G. Mautner (eds) *Language and the Market* (pp. 44–55). Basingstoke: Palgrave-MacMillan.

Lorente, B.P. (2012) The making of "Workers of the World": Language and the language brokerage state. In A. Duchêne and M. Heller (eds) *Language in Late Capitalism: Pride and Profit* (pp. 183–206). New York: Routledge.

Lorente, B.P. (2017) *Scripts of Servitude: Language, Labor Migration and Transnational Domestic Work*. Bristol: Multilingual Matters.

Lutz, H. (2007) Editorial, special issue on domestic work. *European Journal of Women's Studies* 14 (3), 187–192.

Lutz, H. (2011) *The New Maids: Transnational Women and the Care Economy*. New York: Zed Books Ltd.

Madison, D.S. (2012) *Critical Ethnography: Method, Ethics, and Performance*. London: Sage.

Magro, J.L. (2016) Talking hip-hop: When stigmatized language varieties become prestige varieties. *Linguistics and Education* 36, 16–26.

Makoni, S. and Pennycook, A. (eds) (2007) *Disinventing and Reconstituting Languages*. Clevedon: Multilingual Matters.

Malakoff, M. and Hakuta, K. (1991) Translation skill and metalinguistic awareness in bilinguals. In E. Bialystok (ed.) *Language Processing in Bilingual Children* (pp. 141–166). Cambridge: Cambridge University Press.

Malinowski, B. (1922/2014) *Argonauts of the Western Pacific: An Account of Native Enterprise and Adventure in the Archipelalgoes of Melanesian New Guinea*. New York: Routledge.

Mandell, B. and Pherwani, S. (2003) Relationship between emotional intelligence and transformational leadership style: A gender comparison. *Journal of Business and Psychology* 17 (3), 387–404.

Marcus, G.E. (1995) Ethnography in/of the world system: The emergence of multi-sited ethnography. *Annual Review of Anthropology* 24 (1), 95–117.

Martin-Jones, M. and Martin, D. (eds) (2017) *Researching Multilingualism: Critical and Ethnographic Perspectives*. Abingdon: Routledge.

Martín Rojo, L.M. (2013) (De)capitalising students through linguistic practices. A comparative analysis of new educational programmes in a global era. In A. Duchêne, M. Moyer and C. Roberts (eds) *Language, Migration and Social Inequalities: A Critical Sociolinguistic Perspective on Institutions and Work* (pp. 118–146). Bristol: Multilingual Matters.

Martín Rojo, L. (2018) Neoliberalism and linguistic governmentality. In J.W. Tollefson and M. Perez-Milans (eds) *The Oxford Handbook of Language Policy and Planning* (pp. 544–567). Oxford: Oxford University Press.

Martín Rojo, L. (2020) The "self-made speaker": The neoliberal governance of speakers. In L. Martín Rojo and A. Del Percio (eds) *Language and Neoliberal Governmentality* (pp. 91–109). New York: Routledge.

Martín Rojo, L. and Del Percio, A. (eds) (2020) *Language and Neoliberal Governmentality*. New York: Routledge.

Mason, J. (2002) *Qualitative Researching* (2nd edn). London: Sage Publications.

Massey, D. (2013) Vocabularies of the economy. *Soundings: A Journal of Politics and Culture* 54, 9–22.
Matras, Y. (2009) *Language Contact*. Cambridge: Cambridge University Press.
McAdams, D.P. (2001) The psychology of life stories. *Review of General Psychology* 5 (2), 100–122.
McAll, C. (2003) Language dynamics in the bi- and multilingual workplace. In R. Bayley and R.S. Schecter (eds) *Language Socialization in Bilingual and Multilingual Societies* (pp. 235–250). Clevedon: Multilingual Matters.
McDowell, L. and Dyson, J. (2011) The other side of the knowledge economy: 'Reproductive' employment and affective labours in Oxford. *Environment and Planning A: Economy and Space* 43 (9), 2186–2201.
McElhinny, B. (2015) Language and political economy. In N. Bonvillain (ed.) *The Routledge Handbook of Linguistic Anthropology* (pp. 279–300). New York: Routledge.
Mead, M. (1928) *Coming of Age in Samoa*. New York: Marrow.
Mead, M. (1930) *Growing Up in New Guinea*. New York: Blue Ribbon Books.
Meinhof, U.H. and Triandafyllidou, A. (2006) Beyond the diaspora: Transnational practices as transcultural capital. In U.H. Meinhof and A. Triandafyllidou (eds) *Transcultural Europe*. London: Palgrave Macmillan.
Melo-Pfeifer, S. (2022) Linguistic landscapes in the home: Multilingual children's toys, books and games. In A. Stavans and U. Jessner (eds) *Cambridge Handbook of Childhood Multilingualism* (pp. 605–622). Cambridge: Cambridge University Press.
Miller, E.R. (2016) The ideology of learner agency and the neoliberal self. *International Journal of Applied Linguistics* 26 (3), 348–365.
Milroy, L. (1980) *Language and Social Networks*. Oxford: Basil Blackwell.
Mondada, L. (2022) Appealing to the senses: Approaching, sensing, and interacting at the market's stall. *Discourse & Communication* 16 (2), 160–199.
Moyer, M. (2018) Language, mobility, and work. *Language and Intercultural Communication* 18 (4), 357–361.
Nixon, P., Harrington, M. and Parker, D. (2012) Leadership performance is significant to project success or failure: A critical analysis. *International Journal of Productivity and Performance Management* 61 (2), 204–216.
Noblit, G.W. (2004) Storytelling as ethnographic representation. In G.W. Noblit, S.Y. Flores and E.G. Murillo Jr (eds) *Postcritical Ethnography: Reinscribing Critique* (pp. 307–317). Cresskill, NJ: Hampton Press.
North, A. (2017) What kind of literacy? Reflections on the experiences of migrant domestic workers negotiating learning in London. *European Education* 49 (2–3), 184–200.
North, A. (2018) Domestic work, learning and literacy practices across transnational space. *International Studies in Sociology of Education* 27 (2–3), 217–238.
Nortier, J. and Dorleijn, M. (2008) A Moroccan accent in Dutch: A socio-cultural style restricted to the Moroccan community? *International Journal of Bilingualism* 12 (1–2), 125–143.
Norton, B. (2000) *Identity and Language Learning: Gender, Ethnicity and Educational Change*. Essex: Pearson.
Norton, B. (2013) *Identity and Language Learning: Extending the Conversation* (2nd edn). Bristol: Multilingual Matters.
Novoa, A. (2015) Mobile ethnography: Emergence, techniques and its importance to geography. *Human Geographies* 9 (1), 97–107.
Ogbor, J.O. (2000) Mythicizing and reification in entrepreneurial discourse: Ideology critique of entrepreneurial studies. *Journal of Management Studies* 37 (5), 605–635.
Ortner, S.B. (1989) Cultural politics: Religious activism and ideological transformation among 20th century sherpas. *Dialectical Anthropology* 14 (3), 197–211.
Ortner, S. (2006) *Anthropology and Social Theory: Culture, Power, and the Acting Subject*. Durham, NC: Duke University Press.
O'Reilly, K. (2009) *Inductive and Deductive: Key Concepts in Ethnography*. London: Sage.
Parreñas, R.S. (2008) *The Force of Domesticity, Filipina Migrants Globalization*. New York: New York University Press.

Parreñas Salazar, R. (2011) *Servants of Globalization: Migration and Domestic Work* (2nd edn). Stanford, CA: Stanford University Press.

Pécoud, A. (2010) What is ethnic in an ethnic economy? *International Review of Sociology* 20 (1), 59–76.

Pedelty, M. (2004) Parachute anthropology? *Anthropological Quarterly* 77 (2), 339–348.

Pennycook, A. (2017) Translanguaging and semiotic assemblages. *International Journal of Multilingualism* 14 (3), 269–282. https://doi.org/10.1080/14790718.2017.1315810.

Pennycook, A. (2018) *Post-Humanist Applied Linguistics*. New York: Routledge.

Pennycook, A. (2022) Critical applied linguistics in the 2020s. *Critical Inquiry in Language Studies*, 1–22.

Pennycook, A. and Otsuji, E. (2015) *Metrolingualism: Language in the City*. New York: Routledge.

Pietikäinen, S. and Kelly-Holmes, H. (eds) (2013) *Multilingualism and the Periphery*. Oxford: Oxford University Press.

Pietikäinen, S., Jaffe, A., Kelly-Holmes, H. and Coupland, N. (2016) *Sociolinguistics from the Periphery: Small Languages in New Circumstances*. Cambridge: Cambridge University Press.

Piller, I. (2002) *Bilingual Couples Talk: The Discursive Construction of Hybridity*. Amsterdam: John Benjamins Publishing Company.

Piller, I. (2017) *Intercultural Communication: A Critical Introduction*. Edinburgh: Edinburgh University Press.

Piller, I. and Lising, L. (2014) Language, employment, and settlement: Temporary meat workers in Australia. *Multilingua: Journal of Cross-Cultural and Interlanguage Communication* 33 (1–2), 35–59.

Portes, A., Guarnizo, L.E. and Haller, W.T. (2002) Transnational entrepreneurs: An alternative form of immigrant economic adaptation. *American Sociological Review* 67 (2), 278–298.

Potowski, K. (ed.) (2010) *Language Diversity in the USA*. Cambridge: Cambridge University Press.

Prashad, V. (2001) *Everybody was Kung Fu Fighting: Afro-Asian Connections and the Myth of Cultural Purity*. Boston, MA: Beacon Press.

Prinsloo, M. (2022) Moving dirt: Relationality and complementarity in domestic work/ers. *Journal of Postcolonial Linguistics* 7, 89–107.

Pujolar, J. (2020) Linguistic entrepreneurship: Neoliberalism, language learning and class. In L. Martín Rojo and A. Del Percio (eds) *Language and Neoliberal Governmentality* (pp. 113–134). New York: Routledge.

Ramos-Zayas, A.Y. (2012) *Street Therapists: Race, Affect and Neoliberal Personhood in Latino Newark*. Chicago, IL: University of Chicago Press.

Rana, M.B. and Elo, M. (2017) Transnational diaspora and civil society actors driving MNE internationalisation: The case of Grameenphone in Bangladesh. *Journal of International Management* 23 (1), 87–106.

Ricento, T. (ed.) (2000) *An Introduction to Language Policy: Theory and Method*. Malden, MA: Blackwell Publishing.

Rickford, J.R. (1999) The Ebonics controversy in my backyard: A sociolinguist's experiences and reflections. *Journal of Sociolinguistics* 3 (2), 267–275.

Rollins, J. (1985) *Between Women: Domestics and Their Employers*. Philadelphia, PA: Temple University Press.

Romero, M. (2002) *Maid in the U.S.A.* New York: Routledge.

Romero, M., Preston, V. and Wenona, G. (eds) (2014) *When Care Work Goes Global: Locating the Social Relations of Domestic Work*. Farnham: Ashgate.

Rubdy, R. and Pillai, A.D. (2022) Foreign domestic workers and the politics of English in Singapore. *Journal of Postcolonial Linguistics* 7, 51–71.

Rutherford, S. (2001) Any difference? An analysis of gender and divisional management styles in a large airline. *Gender, Work and Organization* 8 (3), 326–345.

Rydell, M. and Hanell, L. (2022) Language for work and work for language: Linguistic aspirations in the marketing of domestic work. *International Journal of the Sociology of Language* 275, 89–109.
Rymes, B. (2014) Communicative repertoire. In C. Leung and B.V. Street (eds) *The Routledge Handbook of English Language Studies*. New York: Routledge.
Sabaté i Dalmau, M. (2013) Fighting exclusion from the margins: Locutorios as sites of social agency and resistance for migrants. In A. Duchêne, M. Moyer and C. Roberts (eds) *Language, Migration and Social Inequalities: A Critical Sociolinguistic Perspective on Institutions and Work* (pp. 248–271). Bristol: Multilingual Matters.
Schluter, A. (2020) Measuring the effectiveness of theory in action: Grass-roots initiatives and social justice for Japan's Kurdish migrants. *Language and Intercultural Communication* 2 (20), 167–180.
Schluter, A. (2021) Language practices through the lens of the neoliberal imaginary in Kurdish-owned eating establishments in Istanbul. In K. Gonçalves and H. Kelly-Holmes (eds) *Language, Global Mobilities, Blue-Collar Workers and Blue-Collar Workplaces*. Abingdon: Routledge.
Schneider, B. (2018) Lobster, tourism and other kinds of business. Economic opportunity and language choice in a multilingual village in Belize. *Language and Intercultural Communication* 18 (4), 390–407.
Schwartz, A. (2006) The teaching and culture of household Spanish: Understanding racist reproduction in 'domestic' discourse. *Critical Discourse Studies* 2 (3), 107–121.
Scollon, R. and Levine, P. (2004) Multimodal discourse analysis as the confluence of discourse and technology. In R. Scollon and P. Levine (eds) *Discourse and Technology: Multimodal Discourse Analysis* (pp. 1–6). Washington, DC: Georgetown University Press.
Scollon, R. and Scollon, S.W. (2004) *Nexus Analysis: Discourse and the Emerging Internet*. New York: Routledge.
Scott, D.M. (2009) Portuguese Americans' acculturation, socioeconomic integration and amalgamation. *Sociologica, Problemas e Praticas* 6, 41–64.
Scott, K. (2017) *Radical Candor: Be a Kick-Ass Boss Without Losing Your Humanity*. New York: St. Martin's Press.
Serwe, S.K. (2021) Investigating language use in immigrant businesses workplace practices of a Thai massage salon owner in Germany. In K. Gonçalves and H. Kelly-Holmes (eds) *Language, Global Mobilities, Blue-Collar Workers and Blue-Collar Workplaces* (pp. 107–127). Abingdon: Routledge.
Sinek, S. (2014) *Leaders Eat Last: Why Some Teams Pull Together and Others Don't*. London: Penguin.
Sheller, M. and Urry, J. (2006) The new mobilities paradigm. *Environment and Planning A: Economy and Space* 38 (2), 207–226.
Sherman, T. and Homoláč, J. (2020) "My mom works in a restaurant here at the market, so she doesn't need Czech": Managing the (non-acquisition) of the majority language in an ethnolinguistic minority community. *Language Policy*. https://doi.org/10.1007/s10993-019-09520-5.
Sherris, A. and Adami, E. (eds) (2019) *Making Signs, Translanguaging Ethnographies: Exploring Urban, Rural and Educational Spaces*. Bristol: Multilingual Matters.
Söderlundh, H. and Keevallik, L. (2022) Labour mobility across the Baltic Sea: Language brokering at a blue-collar workplace in Sweden. *Language in Society*, 1–22. https://doi.org/10.1017=S0047404522000392.
Sommer, E. and Gamper, M. (2018) Transnational entrepreneurial activities: A qualitative network study of self-employed migrants from the former Soviet Union in Germany. *Social Networks* 53, 136–147.
Sorrells, K. (2016) *Intercultural Communication: Globalization and Social Justice* (vol. 2). Thousand Oaks, CA: SAGE Publications.
Spotti, M., Kroon, S. and Li, J. (2019) New speakers of new and old languages: An investigation into the gap between language practices and language policy. *Language Policy* 18, 535–551.

Springer, S., Birch, K. and Macleavy, J. (eds) (2016) *The Handbook of Neoliberalism*. London: Routledge.
Stell, G. and Dragojevic, M. (2017) Multilingual accommodation in Namibia: An examination of six ethnolinguistic groups' language in intra- and intergroup interactions. *Journal of Language and Social Psychology* 36 (2), 167–187.
Streeck, J., Goodwin, C. and LeBaron, C. (2011) Embodied interaction in the material world: An introduction. In J. Streeck, C. Goodwin and C. LeBaron (eds) *Embodied Interactions: Language and Body in the Material World* (pp. 1–26). Cambridge: Cambridge University Press.
Strömmer, M. (2016) Affordances and constraints: Second language learning in cleaning work. *Multilingua Journal of Cross-Cultural and Interlanguage Communication* [Special Issue] 35 (6), 697–721.
Strömmer, M. (2021) Intensified and insecure work of mobile cleaners: Tracing temporal cycles of seasonal cleaning work in a booming tourism destination. In K. Gonçalves and H. Kelly-Holmes (eds) *Language, Global Mobilities, Blue-Collar Workers and Blue-Collar Workplaces* (pp. 187–203). New York: Routledge.
Sultana, S. and Dovchin, S. (2020) Relocalization in digital language practices of university students in Asian peripheries: Critical awareness in a language classroom. *Linguistics and Education* 62, 1–10.
Sunaoshi, Y. (2005) Historical context and intercultural communication: Interactions between Japanese and American factory workers in the American South. *Language in Society* 34 (2), 185–218.
Tang, S. and Kan, H. (2019) Parents, migrant domestic workers and children's speaking of a second language: Evidence from Hong Kong. *Pacific Economic Review* 24 (1), 158–181.
Tarrow, S. (2005) *The New Transnational Activism*. Cambridge: Cambridge University Press.
Thapa, C.B. (2019) Identity and investment in learning English and Chinese: An ethnographic inquiry of two Nepali students in Hong Kong. In J. Gube and F. Gao (eds) *Education, Ethnicity, and Equity in the Multilingual Asian Context* (pp. 33–49). Singapore: Springer Singapore.
Theodoropoulou, I. (2020) Blue-collar workplace communicative practices: A case study in construction sites in Qatar. *Language Policy* 19, 363–387.
Thomas, J. (1993) *Doing Critical Ethnography: Qualitative Research Methods* (vol. 26). Newbury Park: SAGE Publications.
Thurlow, C. (ed.) (2020) *The Business of Words. Wordsmiths, Linguists and Other Language Workers*. New York: Routledge.
Thurlow, C. (2023) Working beside/s words: A case study in the partiality and provinciality of language. *Multimodality & Society*. https://doi.org/10.1177/26349795231202250.
Thurlow, C. and Jaworski, A. (2014) 'Two hundred ninety-four': Remediation and multimodal performance in tourist placemaking. *Journal of Sociolinguistics* 18 (4), 459–494.
Tse, L. (1995) Language brokering among Latino adolescents: Prevalence, attitudes, and school performance. *Hispanic Journal of Behavioral Sciences* 17 (2), 180–193.
Tse, L. (1996) Language brokering in a linguistic communities: The case of Chinese- and Vietnamese-American students. *The Bilingual Research Journal* 20 (3), 485–498.
Urciuoli, B. (2008) Skills and selves in the new workplace. *American Ethnologist* 35 (2), 211–228.
Urry, J. (2007) *Mobilities*. Cambridge: Polity.
Uzzi, B. (1997) Social structure and competition in interfirm networks: The paradox of embeddedness. *Administrative Science Quarterly* 42 (1), 35–67.
Valencia, R.R. (2010) *Dismantling Contemporary Deficit Thinking: Educational Thought and Practice*. Abingdon: Routledge. https://doi.org/10.4324/9780203853214.
Van Mensel, L. (2020) Multilingual family practices: An interactional study. In G. Caliendo, R. Janssens, S. Slembrouck and P. Van Avermaet (eds) *Urban Multilingualism Europe: Bridging the Gap between Language Policies and Language Practices* (pp. 141–163). Berlin: Mouton De Gruyter.

Verschueren, J.F. (1979) What people say they do with words. PhD Dissertation, University of California, Berkeley.
Vessey, R. (2019) Domestic work = language work? Language and gender ideologies in the marketing of multilingual domestic workers in London. *Gender & Language* 13 (3), 314–338.
Vessey, R. and Nicolai, E. (2022) The language ideologies of multilingual nannies in London. *Journal of Sociolinguistics* 27 (3), 221–244.
Vigouroux, C.B. (2013) Informal economy and language practice in the context of migrations. In A. Duchêne, M. Moyer and C. Roberts (eds) *Language, Migration, and Social Inequalities: A Critical Sociolinguistic Perspective on Institutions and Work* (pp. 225–247). Bristol: Multilingual Matters.
Vigouroux, C.B. and Mufwene, S.S. (2020) *Bridging Linguistics and Economics*. Cambridge: Cambridge University Press.
Vine, B. (2004) *Getting Things Done at Work: The Discourse of Power in Workplace Interaction*. Amsterdam: John Benjamins.
Vine, B. (2009) Directives at work: Exploring the contextual complexity of workplace directives. *Journal of Pragmatics* 41, 1395–1405.
Vitale, A. (2011) Linguistic attitudes and use of mother tongue among Spanish speakers in Japan. *The Japan Journal of Multilingualism and Multiculturalism* 17 (1), 30–45.
Wang, V. (2021) For Hong Kong's domestic workers during Covid, discrimination is its own epidemic. *New York Times*, 18 May. See https://www.nytimes.com/2021/05/18/world/asia/hong-kong-domestic-worker-discrimination.html?searchResultPosition=3 (accessed 20 July 2021).
Warriner, D.S. (2007) Transnational literacies: Immigration, language learning and identity. *Linguistics and Education* 18 (3), 201–214.
Weisskirch, R.S. (2013) Family relationships, self-esteem, and self-efficacy among language brokering Mexican American emerging adults. *Journal of Child and Family Studies* 22, 1147–1155.
Wenger, E. (1998) *Communities of Practice: Learning, Meaning, and Identity*. Cambridge: Cambridge University Press.
Williams, C.C. and Nadin, S.J. (2013) Beyond the entrepreneur as a heroic figurehead of capitalism: Re-representing the lived practices of entrepreneurs. *Entrepreneurship & Regional Development* 25 (7–8), 552–568.
Williams, Q., Deumart, A. and Milani, T.M. (eds) (2022) *Struggles for Multilingualism and Linguistic Citizenship*. Bristol: Multilingual Matters.
Wilson, T.D. (1998) Weak ties, strong ties: Network principles in Mexican migration. *Human Organization* 57 (4), 394–403.
Wolfe, J. (2020) Domestic workers are at risk during the coronavirus crisis. Data show most domestic workers are black, Hispanic, or Asian women. *Economic Policy Institute*, 8 April. See https://www.epi.org/blog/domestic-workers-are-at-risk-during-the-coronavirus-crisis-data-show-most-domestic-workers-are-black-hispanic-or-asian-women/ (accessed September 2020).
Wolfram, W. (1993) Ethical considerations in language awareness programs. *Issues in Applied Linguistics* 4 (2), 225–255.
Wright, L. and Higgins, C. (2022) *Diversifying Family Language Policy: Diverse Families, Modalities, Speakers, and Contexts*. Camden: Bloomsbury.
Yeates, N. (2009) *Globalizing Care Economies and Migrant Workers. Explorations in Global Care Chains*. Basingstoke: Palgrave Macmillan.
Zentella, A.C. (1997) *Growing Up Bilingual: Puerto Rican Children in New York*. Oxford: Blackwell.

Index

Access (to participants and/or the research site) 10, 27, 28, 30, 31, 38, 56, 115, 116, 119, 120
   unfettered access/unrestricted access 30, 31, 115, 120
Accommodation/Communication Accommodation Theory 13, 22, 69, 80, 82, 87, 89, 90, 92, 93, 94, 107, 117, 121, 123, 124, 127, 128
   convergence 90, 94, 98, 118
Adami, A. 101, 102, 108, 111, 113, 123, 140
Affective Attachment 97
Agency/Agentive 40, 48, 66, 72, 75, 76, 90, 97, 98, 110, 116, 119, 122
Ahearn, L.M. 40, 98, 129
Androutsopoulos, J. 110, 111, 129
Anglophone customer 1, 4, 11, 22, 25, 40, 108, 110, 112, 113, 114, 117, 122, 123, 128
Appadurai, A. 7, 129
Artifacts/Objects (as artifacts)/material(ity) 2, 20, 35, 37, 48, 71, 73, 75, 100, 104, 105, 106, 111, 113

Backstage (in terms of Goffman's [1959] front stage/back stage distinction) 9, 47
Belonging 80, 81, 97, 116
Block, D. 7, 45, 54, 98, 130
Bourdieu, P. 4, 19, 20, 81, 86, 87, 98, 130, 133
Blackledge, A. 103, 108, 130
Blommaert, J. 2, 7, 9, 32, 67, 81, 101, 102, 108, 111, 113, 123, 130
Bucholtz, M. 19, 22, 100, 102, 113

Cameron, D. 28, 32, 85, 130
Canagarajah, S. 6, 7, 19, 50, 97, 101, 106, 130, 131
Capital (in the Bourdieusian, 1991 sense) 3, 20, 21, 48, 63, 64, 68, 70, 77, 79, 80, 81, 82, 83, 85, 86, 87, 93, 94, 97, 98, 110, 112, 121, 122
   cultural capital 3, 48, 68, 82, 85, 87, 121
   economic capital 81, 83, 85, 86, 87, 110, 121
   social capital 20, 81, 86, 121
   symbolic capital 64, 77, 110
   transcultural capital 87
Care work 5, 6, 7, 8, 38
   domestic work/domestic labor/domestic workers 1, 2, 3, 4, 5, 6, 7, 8, 9, 10, 11, 20, 22, 25, 28, 29, 33, 36, 38, 39, 41, 42, 44, 46, 50, 54, 61, 62, 64, 76, 100, 113, 114, 122, 124, 125, 126, 127, 128
   transnational domestic workers 2
   nanny/childcare 41, 44, 45, 76
   elderly care 6, 81, 87, 96
   domestic workers in the US 10
Carvahlo, A.M. 20, 131
Castels, S. 6
Citizenship 11, 15, 139
Community of Practice 82, 84, 93, 94, 95, 105, 106, 111, 115, 120
Commodify/Commodification of language 8, 85, 103
Cook, V. 63, 100, 102, 110, 112, 122, 124
Co-Present Immersion 34
Coupland, N. 101, 102, 130, 131, 139

Creese, A. 103, 108, 130
Customer-employee communication/ customer-employee interaction/company-external communication 40, 71, 76, 111, 114, 123, 124, 127
Critical-constructivist sociolinguistics 2, 32

Darvin, R. 80, 82, 94, 96, 97, 98, 110, 112, 121, 122
Decapitalization 21, 22, 80, 81, 82, 83, 85, 94, 99, 122, 124
DeCosta, P.I 81, 87, 96, 117
Deliberate deception 28, 30
Diaspora 80, 82, 85, 86, 87, 95, 96, 97, 98, 120, 121
Digital translation 109, 110, 112
Dual-linguality 78, 84, 87, 88, 89, 90, 91
Duchêne, A. 7, 73, 87, 98, 103, 114, 129, 131, 132, 137, 139, 142

Embodied/embodiment (as part of embodied communication/ embodied sociolinguistics) 1, 4, 19, 22, 100, 102, 106, 108, 109, 111, 113, 124, 128
Emotional Intelligence/Emotionally intelligent 2, 21, 25, 40, 41, 44, 47, 48, 50, 51, 53, 54, 55, 56, 57, 59, 61, 63, 76, 77, 117, 118, 120
English 2, 4, 8, 12, 13, 14, 15, 19, 20, 22, 24, 29, 30, 31, 45, 46, 47, 48, 57, 63, 64, 65, 66, 69, 70, 72, 73, 77, 79, 82, 88, 96, 100, 101, 102, 103, 104, 105
  English-language competence 48, 79, 82, 113, 117, 124
  limited English-language proficiency 13, 20, 70
Ethnographic research/ethnography 20, 21, 27, 29, 32, 33, 34, 35, 36, 37, 38, 39, 116
  critical ethnography 32, 36, 37, 39
  mobile ethnography 21, 32, 33, 34, 35
  post-critical ethnography 27, 32, 33, 36, 37, 39

García, O. xiii, xiv, 46, 101, 133
Galloway, L. 50, 52, 61, 133

Giddens, A. 6, 34, 38, 133, 134
Global Care Chain 5, 6, 114
Goffman, E. 9, 47, 133
Goldstein, T. 19, 30, 65, 82, 99, 113, 133
Goleman, D. xi, 21, 41, 52, 53, 54, 55, 56, 58, 59, 61, 76, 119, 133
Gonçalves, K. xi, 1, 2, 4, 5, 6, 7, 8, 9, 10, 12, 19, 22, 23, 24, 25, 27, 31, 32, 33, 36, 38, 40, 41, 44, 46, 51, 56, 58, 59, 84, 85, 86, 87, 88, 89, 96, 101, 102, 112, 113, 114, 115, 128, 132, 133, 134, 140, 141
Goodwin, C. 101, 134, 141
Grillo, R.D. 19, 117, 123, 134
Gumperz, J. 4, 19, 134

Hall, K. 19, 22, 100, 102, 113
Heller, M. xiv, 7, 29, 33, 38, 85, 103, 114, 132, 134, 137
Hidden spaces/hidden domains 10, 22
Hochschild, A.R. 5, 6, 8, 11, 25, 77, 134
Holmes, J. xiii, xiv, 31, 50, 134, 135
Home (as a workplace) 5, 6, 9, 17, 36, 45, 61, 76, 77, 78, 105
Horizontal assimilation 21, 79, 98, 121
Hovens, D. 112, 114, 128, 134
Hymes, D. 101, 134

Informal labor/informal sector/informal domain 5, 82, 114
Inter-employee communication 3, 82
ILO (International Labour Organization) 5, 9, 10
Investment – as a concept introduced by Norton (2000) and advanced by Darvin and Norton (2015) 21, 22, 80, 82, 94, 109, 110, 111, 113, 120, 121, 122
Identity 12, 14, 21, 50, 79, 80, 81, 85, 94, 95, 96, 97, 98, 121, 122
Imagined identity 97, 121
Ideology 22, 79, 80, 94, 97, 121, 122

Jacquemet, M. 100, 110, 135
Johnstone, B. xiv, 27, 34, 115, 135

Kaiper-Marquez, A. xiv, 1, 5, 7, 8, 31, 38, 114, 127, 128, 135

Keevalik, L. 50, 64, 112, 128
Kelly-Holmes, H. xiii, xiv, 94, 98, 112, 113, 114, 128, 132, 133, 137, 139, 140, 141
Kleifgen, J.A. 82, 99, 106, 113, 128, 135
Kramsch, C. 19, 86, 94, 135
Kusters, A. 2, 4, 19, 22, 101, 102, 109, 113, 135

Ladegaard, H. xiv, 6, 8, 9, 10, 31, 33, 114, 135, 136
Language brokers/language brokering 22, 47, 63, 64, 69, 70, 71, 72, 77, 87, 101, 104, 110, 116, 117, 123, 126, 127, 128
    inter-employee brokering 40, 56, 67, 68, 69, 77, 118
Language ideology/language ideologies 1, 22
Language Policy 1, 9, 44, 63, 65, 67, 69, 71, 73, 84, 112, 116, 117, 118
Lanza, E. xiv, 9, 36, 44, 136
Leadership style 2, 21, 40, 41, 48, 51, 52, 53, 61, 76
Legitimated domination 19, 71, 117, 123
Levon, E. 27, 32, 136
Lexander, K.V. xiv, 111, 129
Lorente, B. XIV, 1, 5, 6, 8, 10, 25, 31, 38, 46, 103, 122, 127, 128, 136, 137
Lutz, H. 5, 6, 8, 25, 38, 137

Magda's softer side 21, 40, 50, 76
Madison, D.S. 33, 36, 37, 137
Makoni, S. xiv, 1, 5, 7, 8, 31, 38, 46, 114, 127, 135, 137
Malinowski, B. 37, 137
Marcus, G.E. 33, 34, 137
Marginalization/marginalized 7, 9, 37, 82, 116
Martin-Jones, M. xiv, 33, 36, 116, 130, 137
Martín-Rojo, L. 21, 46, 48, 80, 81, 85, 94, 117, 122, 124, 137
Massey, D. 26, 138
McAdams, D.P. 41, 137
McElhinny, B. 7, 101, 134, 138
Mead, M. 34, 138
Migrant entrepreneurship 22, 86, 116, 118, 120, 128

Migrant women 1, 3, 5, 6, 24, 33
Mondada, L. 106, 138
Moyer, M. 20, 21, 80, 81, 85, 94, 122, 124, 129, 131, 132, 134, 136, 137, 138, 139, 142
Multicompetence 22, 68, 100, 101, 102, 103, 106, 109, 116, 117, 122, 123, 124, 127, 128
Multilingual blue-collar/blue-collar workplace/multilingual workplace 1, 3, 6, 9, 20, 21, 22, 44, 48, 50, 51, 52, 56, 64, 77, 82, 94, 99, 103, 112, 113, 114, 115, 117, 118, 121, 123, 127, 128
Multilingual Communities 19
Multimodality 1, 4, 19, 82, 100, 102, 103, 104, 105, 106, 107, 108, 110, 111, 113, 122, 124

Neoliberalism/neoliberal 7, 21, 45, 80, 81, 85, 87, 103
    neolberal capital flows 21, 80
Network/Social network 9, 50, 53, 64, 81, 82, 86, 87, 96, 97, 98, 121, 122
New Jersey 1, 11, 13, 14, 15, 20, 31, 44, 46, 47, 48, 56, 57, 80, 87, 96, 112, 124
    Elizabeth 4, 11, 13, 14, 15, 20, 36, 46, 47, 48, 49, 57
    Newark 4, 11, 15, 20, 21, 22, 36, 44, 46, 79, 80, 81, 84, 85, 86, 87, 89, 96, 98, 104, 126
    Newark's Ironbound district/(The) Ironbound 11, 12, 13, 14, 15, 16, 20, 23, 36, 79, 81, 82, 83, 85, 86, 87, 89, 91, 93, 94, 95, 96, 97, 99, 100, 104, 120, 121, 123
New division of labor 5, 7
Noblit, G.W. 33, 36, 37, 138
Norton, B. 46, 80, 82, 94, 96, 97, 98, 110, 112, 121, 122, 131, 132, 138
Novoa, A. 33, 35, 138

Otsuji, E. 2, 4, 19, 32, 114, 139

Participation-while-interviewing 35
Pécoud, A. 86, 112, 138
Pennycook, A. 2, 22, 32, 33, 100, 102, 113, 122

Pietikäinen, S. xiv, 33, 94, 98, 134, 139
Piller, I. 9, 19, 78, 84, 88, 112, 114, 139
Portuguese 1, 2, 3, 11, 12, 13, 14, 15, 19, 20, 22, 29, 30, 31, 40, 44, 45, 46, 47, 51, 56, 57, 58, 63, 64, 65, 66, 67, 68, 69, 70, 76, 77, 79, 80, 81, 83, 84, 85, 86, 87, 88, 89, 90, 91, 92, 93, 94, 95, 96, 97, 98, 99, 100, 104, 105, 107, 109, 112, 114, 117, 118, 120, 121, 122, 123, 124, 127, 128
Positionality 22, 27, 36, 37, 85, 86, 94, 97, 98, 116, 120, 121, 122, 128
Post-Humanist Applied Linguistics 1, 22, 100, 113, 122
Poststructuralist 2, 32, 36
Power 1, 8, 19, 20, 26, 30, 40, 51, 62, 63, 66, 68, 71, 72, 73, 74, 75, 76, 77, 81, 85, 87, 93, 94, 96, 98, 110, 114, 116, 117, 118, 119, 120, 121, 123
　asymmetric power/inequality/ inequalities 1, 7, 8, 10, 20, 32, 40, 42, 93, 94, 98
　production of/maintenance of inequality 8, 73, 92, 112
Privilege 3, 7, 20
Prashad, V. 21, 79, 98, 121, 139

Reflexivity 36
Researcher positionality 22, 27, 36, 37, 128
Rymes, B. 4, 101
Rollins, J. 8, 28, 29, 30, 38, 139
Romero, M. 5, 7, 8, 25, 114, 139

Schluter, A. xi, 1, 2, 4, 5, 6, 7, 8, 10, 19, 24, 25, 31, 36, 38, 40, 51, 56, 58, 59, 85, 87, 88, 89, 94, 96, 97, 114, 116, 122, 129, 131, 133, 140

Scollon R. & Scollon, S.W. 100, 106, 110, 111, 140
Scott, K. 59, 61, 140
Second-shift(s) (Hochschild, 1989) 11, 77
Semiotic repertoire(s)/semiotic resources/ semiotic assemblages 4, 20, 22, 32, 101, 102, 103, 106, 108, 113
Serwe, S. 19, 86, 112, 128, 140
Sheller, M. 33, 140
Sherris, E. 101, 102, 108, 111, 113, 123, 140
Sinek, S. 31, 50, 51, 120, 127, 140
Social justice 32, 33
Social practice (language as a) 2, 32
Socio-economic mobility/upward mobility 29, 64, 113, 124, 128
Söderlundh, H. 50, 64, 114, 140
Spanish 3, 4, 13, 14, 15, 31, 40, 47, 65, 66, 67, 69, 76, 80, 82, 84, 88, 89, 90, 91, 92, 93, 94, 95, 96, 98, 104, 112, 117
Symbolic value of languages 1, 3, 112

Thapa, C.B. 111, 141
Theodoropoulou, I. 2, 19, 32, 141
Thurlow, C. xiv, 9, 102, 114, 141
Transidioma 100, 110
Translanguaging 102, 110, 122
Tse, L. 63, 64, 141

Uptake 108, 111
Urry, J. 7, 33, 35, 136, 140, 141

Vigouroux, C. 82, 83, 86, 122, 142
Vine, B. 40, 63, 66, 110, 134, 137, 140, 142
Vulnerable 2, 5, 6, 7, 8, 10, 28, 29, 30, 32, 33, 116

Wenger, E. 82, 94, 106, 136, 142

For Product Safety Concerns and Information please contact our EU Authorised Representative:

Easy Access System Europe

Mustamäe tee 50

10621 Tallinn

Estonia

gpsr.requests@easproject.com

www.ingramcontent.com/pod-product-compliance
Ingram Content Group UK Ltd.
Pitfield, Milton Keynes, MK11 3LW, UK
UKHW010140181125
3613IPUK00006B/77